the FAMILY-FRIENDLY CHURCH

by
Ben Freudenburg
with
Rick Lawrence

Group
Loveland, Colorado

Ben:

I dedicate this work to my wife Jennifer and my daughters Cori and Sara. Their love, patience, dedication, and inspiration gave me the courage and permission to produce this work. They continue to teach me what it means to be a husband and father.

Rick:

To Beverly Rose—all my journeys lead to you.

The Family-Friendly Church

Credits

Editors: Bob Buller and Dave Thornton
Chief Creative Officer: Joani Schultz
Copy Editor: Julie Meiklejohn
Art Director: Ray Tollison
Cover Art Director: Jeff A. Storm
Designer: Randall Miller Designs
Computer Graphic Artist: Theresa Mesa
Cover Illustrator: Otto Pfannschmidt
Illustrator: Matt Wood
Production Manager: Gingar Kunkel

Unless otherwise noted, Scripture taken from the HOLY BIBLE, NEW INTERNATIONAL VERSION®. Copyright © 1973, 1978, 1984 by International Bible Society. Used by permission of Zondervan Publishing House. All rights reserved.

Library of Congress Cataloging-in-Publication Data
Freudenburg, Ben F., 1950-
      The family friendly church / by Ben Freudenburg, with Rick Lawrence.
            p. cm.
      Includes bibliographical references.
      ISBN 0-7644-2048-8 (alk. paper)
      1. Church work with families. 2. Christian education—Home training. I. Lawrence, Rick, 1961- . II. Title.
      BV4438.F76 1998
      259'.1—dc21   98-16144
10 9 8 7   07 06 05 04 03 02   CIP
Printed in the United States of America.
Visit our Web site: www.grouppublishing.com

Contents

Acknowledgments

Ben:

This work is a reflection of the people God has placed in my life and the places he has sent me. They have helped unveil to me a new vision for his ministry. Special thanks to those whose partnership in this project made it possible:

I thank Pastor Vern Gundermann for his leadership, support, and vision for this project and Concordia Lutheran Church and its staff for giving up ministry time and taking on additional workloads to support this work.

I will always be grateful to my partner, friend, and expert editor Rick Lawrence, whose gifts in making the printed word sing with meaning and power and whose dedicated heart for Christ and love for kids powered his dedication and partnership in seeing this work to completion.

I am indebted to Thom and Joani Schultz and Group Publishing, who initiated a special partnership to write this work, giving time and talent for the sake of Christ, his kids, and the gospel.

And to Les Stroh, my mentor and friend, whose encouragement, vision, and coaching gave direction and encouragement to begin this journey.

I also give thanks to God for all who gave me entrance into their busy lives to share their hopes, dreams, passions, and ideas for the role of families in the kingdom of Christ:

I grew much from and am thankful for Roger Charman at Focus on the Family; Dr. Merton Strommen, the founder of Search Institute and the Augsburg Youth and Family Institute; and Eugene Roehlkepartain of Search Institute.

I gained valuable insights into family-friendly ministry from the congregations and staffs of Cherry Creek Presbyterian Church in Aurora, Colorado; Village Seven Presbyterian Church and Holy Cross Church in Colorado Springs, Colorado; Our Father Lutheran Church in Littleton, Colorado; Holy Nativity Church and Zion Anoka Church in Minneapolis, Minnesota; St. Michael's Church and St. Luke's Church in Bloomington, Minnesota; Zion Church in Belleville, Illinois; and St. John's Church in Arnold, Missouri.

I'm also thankful for the many teachers, professional counselors, and district executives for youth and education in the Lutheran Church Missouri Synod who gave me helpful information and personal insights.

And many thanks to a small band of youth workers—Kevin

Pigg, Mark Piel, Jill Hasstedt, Nancy Going, and Rob Rose—whose energy, interest, and support through a one-year study group furthered the pursuit of this home-centered, church-supported family ministry model.

Finally, thanks to the pastors, teachers, professional church workers, and lay people all over the country who've experienced the workshop that planted the seeds for this book. Their help in shaping the final content through their feedback, questions, and phone calls was invaluable.

Rick:

Thanks to Ben and Jennifer for opening your hearts, your home, your history—but not those jars of pickled salmon—to me. The time I spent with you changed my life and my vision for ministry. Thanks to Bev for your love, support, encouragement, and gourmet-meal preparation. Thanks to Mike Warden and Joani Schultz for suggesting this partnership. And thanks to my magazine team members for their support, feedback, and occasionally bizarre repartee–you helped keep me sane.

Journey Preparation

This book is the chronicle of an exciting journey that changed my life and my approach to ministry in the church. But it's more than simply a retelling of what I learned on my journey; it's an explicit invitation for you to join me in a quest to strengthen the partnership between the home and the church. If it happens, the world will be a changed place—a place more impacted by the gospel of Jesus than it is today.

A journey involves more than gathering snapshots. When you venture on a journey, you plunge yourself into a learning experience that has the potential to forever change you. If you choose to let the journey transform you, it can. A simple trip won't accomplish that. Say your goal is to take a sightseeing trip to visit castles in Ireland. Once there, you find your first castle, walk around it, admire its beauty, and take a few pictures. Then you move on to the next castle. If, instead, you're on a *journey* to discover your Irish roots, you would explore that same castle in a whole new way. You'd find out who lived there and what's happened there—the remarkable events in the castle's history that changed people's lives. You might even ask the walls, "If you could talk, what stories would you tell?" Your encounter with the castle would literally have the power to change who you are and what you believe.

In other words, when we go on a journey, we give ourselves permission to encounter new places and people with an open heart and mind—to discover new truths. We look for ways to grow, and we open ourselves to new ways of seeing what we thought we already knew.

On this journey, you have a chance to try a new way of approaching family ministry in the church. Along the way, you'll encounter places to stop, consider, and reflect. You'll find:

1. Rest Stops

—Here you can stop to reflect on the journey so far and think about how it relates to your beliefs and what you do in your home and church.

2. Quiet Detours

—Here you can veer from a focus on your own life and ministry to reconnect with God through word and prayer. These Quiet Detours look remarkably similar to each other, but they all have subtle differences in focus. The similarities emphasize key issues affecting all homes. The differences highlight the changing needs of your home.

3. Construction Zones

—Here you'll stop to work a little—to take what you've learned and actually construct something new for your church.

Use these "journey breaks" to reflect on your own history and beliefs about faith development in the home, to consider how your beliefs impact the church's ministry, and to start shaping new ways to minister to families.

By the end of this journey, you'll have a new passion for partnering with families to accomplish the church's primary mission—fueling the faith development of its people so they can gather those outside its influence into the waiting arms of Christ.

Introduction

A father on his deathbed called his family together. His children—Jerry, Maryann, Margaret, Dorothy—and his pregnant wife Viola gathered close to his bed. He said to them, "I know you're wondering who's going to provide for you, where you'll stay, and how things will work out without me. You must remember the promises of God and keep your eyes focused on Jesus, his cross, and his empty tomb. All will work out."

Somehow, the father just knew Viola was pregnant with a son. So he said, "The boy Mom is carrying—I don't care what name you give to him, but promise me this: that you'll tell him about Jesus. Teach him well, so someday I'll be able to meet my son in heaven."

Soon after, the father died. It was December 26, 1949.

The son was born on April 2, 1950.

The family kept its promise. The mom took her son to be baptized and faithfully taught him about Jesus. She took him to church and Sunday school every week and enrolled him in a Christian school. She taught him by example what it meant to give part of his money to the Lord's work and the importance of daily Bible reading, devotion, and service. She taught him to pray, and she modeled her love and passion for God to him.

On May 18, 1996, that mother started her new life in heaven. I am the boy she was carrying as my father lay dying. Through the power of the Holy Spirit and Mom's active participation in nurturing my faith, my love for Jesus grew and flourished. I love and willingly serve him, and I know I will someday meet my father in heaven.

Rest Stop

Stop to reflect on what you've just read—how it relates to your beliefs and what you do in your home and church.

- Were your parents the most important people in shaping your faith—either positively or negatively? Why or why not?

Think of how you'd explain your answer to a friend.

I know my mom was the most important catalyst in my faith development. I'm guessing your parents played a similar role in one way or another. That should be no surprise. According to Search Institute's landmark report, *Youth in Protestant Churches,* a parent's positive influence on a child's faith development dwarfs all other influences.[1]

I believe God's vision for faith formation is simply this:

> *Parents are the primary Christian educators in the church, and the family is the God-ordained institution for building faith in young people and for passing faith on from one generation to the next.*

Over the years, this vision has been lost in a program-centered church culture in which parents find themselves on the sidelines instead of in the game, shaping their children's faith and lives.

In this book, we're urging churches to shift their programming and structure to a home-centered, church-supported model for nurturing faith. Join us in working out a home-based ministry strategy that will give our kids a better chance to develop a passion for following Jesus.

---

[1] Eugene C. Roehlkepartain and Peter L. Benson, *Youth in Protestant Churches* (Minneapolis, MN: Search Institute, 1993), 25.

Section 1
Sounding the Alarm

As Christians, we don't have to listen too hard to hear alarms going off in our culture and in the church that signal problems in the way our faith is impacting society.

1. Knowledge of Scripture is at an all-time low. According to researcher George Barna, the number of people who read their Bible during a typical week continues a downward spiral—just one out of three say they cracked the Scriptures during the week before Barna's survey.[1] And more than a third of all Americans don't read the Bible because they feel "it's irrelevant to their lives."[2]

2. Our culture no longer embraces God's law. The only commandment still heeded by people in our culture is the eighth commandment—"You shall not steal." You can still go to jail for stealing. But doctors can legally do late-term abortions. Take a look at most political campaigns, and you'll see "giving false testimony" is not even a speed bump. Adultery is just a mildly interesting plot twist on most TV shows. Teachers will tell you that "respect for authority" is at an all-time low. Still-emerging cults remind us all over again that people have plenty of gods to choose from. "Misusing the name of the Lord" is a normal part of our public rhetoric. For many Christians, "remembering the Sabbath" has become a monthly afterthought instead of a weekly commitment (just under half of American adults—45 percent—say they attended a church service during the previous week).[3] As far as the ninth and tenth commandments, our whole consumer culture is driven by coveting people and stuff.

3. The life values of Christian teenagers and adults are often indistinguishable from the world's life values. In survey after survey, the beliefs of Christians are largely the same as the beliefs of non-Christians. For example, when pollster George Barna asked Christian and non-Christian teenagers an array of questions about their moral behavior, their answers mirrored each other:

	Christian	Non-Christian
● Ever watched an X-rated or pornographic movie?	32%	41%
● Ever cheated on a test, exam, or other evaluation?	29%	27%
● Ever had sexual intercourse?	23%	29%[4]

In his book *Absolute Confusion,* George Barna writes, "Religion, although an enduring interest of Americans, remains oddly incapable of influencing the lives of a large number of people."[5] At a time when eight out of ten American adults believe that Jesus was crucified, died, resurrected, and is spiritually alive today...[6]

- four out of ten believe Jesus made mistakes;
- one out of three believes that God is someone other than the perfect, all-powerful, omniscient Creator and Lord described by the Bible;
- three out of five do not believe in Satan;
- about half believe that all religions are basically the same; and
- most cannot name half of the Ten Commandments or who preached the Sermon on the Mount.[7]

4. American families don't realize their power and influence. In a massive 1997 study of American teenagers, researchers discovered that kids who "feel connected to their parents or school were less likely to suffer emotional distress, think about suicide, be violent, smoke cigarettes, drink alcohol, or smoke marijuana." These parent-nurtured kids also tended to delay their first sexual experiences.[8] In another study of fathers' influence on their kids, researchers found the more kids get involved in activities with their dads, the more education they complete and the less they exhibit "delinquent behaviors."[9]

Statistics like these could fill a whole book. And if most teenagers were getting the parent contact they thirst for, we'd be celebrating right now. But in a 1997 Search Institute survey of high school students, 86 percent said they feel disconnected from and devalued by adults, and only 22 percent said they could communicate positively with their own parents.[10]

5. The Christian church has less and less impact in the lives of its members and in the culture itself. According to George Barna in *Absolute Confusion,* nearly two out of three adults contend that "it does not matter what religious faith you follow because all faiths teach similar lessons about life."[11]

As pastors, youth ministers, Christian educators, teachers, and parents, we have four things in common:

- We desperately want everyone we know to trust Christ for salvation.
- We also want people to love God with all their heart, soul, and mind.
- We believe it's very important that people love their neighbors as they love themselves.
- We want these Christian beliefs to be integrated into the everyday lives of people.

Here's the struggle: If that's what we want, but the facts say it's not happening, it's time to listen to the alarms. And maybe the first alarm we should hear is the one sounding in our own homes.

Notes

[1] George Barna, *Absolute Confusion* (Ventura, CA: Regal Books, 1993), 59.

[2] *Bible Reading in America,* a study funded by Tyndale House Publishers (Ventura,CA: Barna Research Group, 1996).

[3] Barna, *Absolute Confusion,* 59.

[4] George Barna, *Generation Next* (Ventura, CA: Regal Books, 1995), 98.

[5] Barna, *Absolute Confusion,* 14.

[6] Ibid., 83.

[7] Ibid., 139.

[8] J. Richard Udry, Journal of the American Medical Association (September 1997).

[9] Victor C. Strasburger, "Tuning in to Teenagers," Newsweek (September 1997).

[10] as reported by Bill Howard, "Assets vs. Risks: The Selling of Rival Youth Development Strategies," Youth Today (September/October 1997), 1.

[11] Barna, *Absolute Confusion,* 73.

Chapter 1
Trouble at Home

In my own life, I heard the alarm loud and clear when I woke up one morning with a mistress. I'd been involved with her my entire adult life, but I had never admitted it. I'd often felt helpless to resist her charms. With the best of intentions, I listened to my guilt and vowed fidelity—only to fall again. Finally, three years ago, that relationship threatened my ministry, my marriage, and all I held most dear.

Before you rush to judgment, understand that I've had a two-decade love affair with the work of the church, my mistress. I found great satisfaction, almost a euphoria, in helping design and carry out programs that spurred faith growth in children and youth. When I saw kids come to Christ; when they felt empowered to use their gifts at church, at school, and at home; when parents told me what a significant role I played in their kids' lives; when I saw kids come back after college to begin shaping the faith of their own families—it gave me a powerful sense of significance: "My life really matters for something." It's thrilling to sense you've somehow been a conduit for the power of God in others' lives.

So what's wrong with all that?

The enticing nature of my work created a harmful imbalance in my personal life. I perpetually gravitated toward the work of the church, and my family, my personal life, and even my own faith suffered. Because I was so driven to please my mistress, I felt tremendous guilt whenever I let her down. If I didn't meet the church's needs—and I mean all its needs—I wrestled with crushing guilt.

What the mistress needed was great programs, personal visits with church members, growing numbers, exciting and meaningful teaching, extravagant fund-raising projects, innovative and "cool" youth activities, a creatively designed vacation Bible school and camp, a family-friendly confirmation program that was better every year, dynamic parent programs, youth-friendly worship, captivating and extensive mission trips, a growing slate of leadership responsibilities at conferences, and increased impact through speaking engagements and writing assignments.

Of course, there's nothing wrong with enjoying your work. But, like any other addicted person, I'd go through withdrawal when I wasn't heeding the mistress' call.

Meanwhile, my determined mission to develop a model ministry to children, youth, and families—to nurture their faith in Christ—was threatening my own family. My relationships with my wife Jennifer and my daughters Cori and Sara were under siege. I'd created a void in our home. I wasn't doing bad things at home; I simply wasn't around—and my family felt seriously cheated.

Now I had two competing guilts—the guilt I felt when I didn't cater to my church mistress and the guilt I felt when I wasn't home "putting my house in order." I thought I knew what God expected of me at home, but I was wrong. What I really knew how to do was work…at church. What I didn't know was that I was burning out.

Physically, I was a wreck. I wasn't happy or productive. I was getting my work done, but I wasn't as creative as I used to be. And I was a little paranoid. Sometimes, when things didn't go well, I thought people were out to sabotage my ministry. Vern Gundermann, my senior pastor, gave me a book on adrenalin and stress, but I discounted it. I sent for audiotapes from Focus on the Family on balancing your life and family. They talked about adrenalin addiction—and they described me. But still it didn't connect.

So I went to see my doctor. He prescribed a vacation. But I turned vacations into work. I tried to have fun, but I would also plan, create, make work phone-calls, and finish projects. I'd brought the mistress with me on vacation.

Finally, after several visits to the doctor, he asked me to consider taking an antidepressant. I thought, "Why would he say that? I'm not depressed." The doctor told me that the lows I was experiencing were caused by a problem with my adrenalin. You know how you have a little letdown after a conference or an event? That's simply the aftermath of an adrenalin high. I lived on adrenalin—so much so that my adrenal gland had nothing left to give most days, plunging me into a perpetual state of adrenalin withdrawal. That's what was causing my lack of energy and creativity.*

The doctor said I was "burning through my allotted years of life faster than the speed of light." He told me Prozac would target the adrenalin in my system and draw it back into my adrenal gland. I told him I didn't want drugs and asked if there was another way to climb out of the hole I'd dug for myself. He said, "Let your body rest so it can naturally rebalance your adrenalin level." So I tried to do that. But I couldn't force myself to take the time I really needed.

That's about the time my wife sat me down and said she was afraid for me: "If you don't change the way we're living our life together, I will have to make a change in our relationship." She left that last part dangling. She simply couldn't go on living with a demanding mistress in our home. And she was afraid my health would

---

* For more in-depth information on adrenalin addiction, read Dr. Archibald D. Hart's book *The Hidden Link Between Adrenalin and Stress* (Word Books).

continue to deteriorate until I literally killed myself. She asked for drastic action because the situation was drastic.

I was deeply concerned after that conversation. I went to see Les Stroh—a close friend and church consultant—and basically barged into his office. I told him what Jennifer had said. I thought he would comfort me and tell me everything was going to be OK. Instead, he asked me about my calendar, listened, and then said, "If your family is so important to you, why doesn't it show up on your calendar? There's nothing there. If family time was really of value to you, it would show up in your actions." Les was right. I felt exposed and uncertain of my path.

Right about then, God intruded into the mess I'd made and offered me a pathway to grace. My church offered to give me a three-month sabbatical to do research on family-centered churches. My first thought was predictably work-related: "What a great opportunity!" But something deeper inside me knew I desperately needed this time to relax, reflect, and rebuild my personal life. What a rare chance to focus on my wife and children—to begin healing those relationships and to find space to heal myself.

So I agreed to take a three-month sabbatical. Really, the "work purpose" of the sabbatical gave me permission to care for myself and my family.

Les Stroh offered to take me to a condominium for several days to help me plan what I would do. I had no idea how to take the first step. But he and I hammered out the rudiments of a plan and a long "to do" list. Just coming up with a plan was healing for me. The focus was on discovering what a family-friendly church looked like, but God had more in mind than that.

Chapter 2
Trouble at Church

At church, all of my work and energy was not producing the faith maturity I expected in the children and teenagers I was responsible for. What difference was I really making? My denomination asked Search Institute, a respected youth research organization in Minnesota, to study youth and adults in the church to discover what qualities of congregational life nurture faith. What they found was stunning...and humbling:

"There is little debate about the importance of family in shaping people's lives, including their physical, intellectual, emotional, psychological, and social development. But we sometimes forget that the family is just as important in the area of spiritual or faith development. This study examined several ways families express faith in the home—each of which is extremely important for nurturing a dynamic faith. Four family practices are particularly important in helping young people grow in faith (both in childhood and adolescence):

1. Talking about faith with your mother.

2. Talking about faith with your father.

3. Having family devotions or prayer.

4. Doing family projects to help other people.

"Fewer than one-third of youth report that any of the above activities happen often—either in their past or present—and adults are even less likely to remember these experiences in their childhood and adolescence. It is hardly surprising, then, that parents—most of whom did not experience nurturing of their faith in their own growing up years—need help nurturing their children's faith."[1]

Why don't churched kids abuse drugs and alcohol less than their unchurched peers? Why do our kids have virtually the same teenage pregnancy rate as unchurched kids? Why don't even our best kids lead lives away from church that are fundamentally different from their friends' lives? If we're really making a difference, why can't we see it in our kids' lives? We've got to do something different or admit that we can't make a difference.

I've wrestled with these questions for twenty-five years. As I reflect on what's led to the vision I have today, I see that God was revealing to me a telltale trail of clues that led to some profound conclusions about the way the church impacts families.

My first youth ministry position was at Shore Haven Lutheran Church in Euclid, Ohio. Jennifer and I quickly assumed the role of surrogate parents to almost 100 kids in the church and community. We took them on picnics, had them over for dinner, planned retreats that were like family vacations, did service projects together, and so on. We had very little parental support, so we took over the parents' role.

And we burned out big time—especially after we had our own kids.

It pains me to say that when we left Shore Haven, many of those kids dropped out of the church. I didn't know what I'd done wrong, but I knew it was bad.

We accepted a call to Our Redeemer Lutheran Church in Hutchison, Kansas. The community's attitude about parents' involvement in their children's lives was completely opposite of Euclid's. The whole community was focused on families. We tried to do our old Euclid-style of youth ministry, but it didn't work. Families were so involved with each other that we weren't expected to be surrogate parents to the church's kids. We had to embrace the community's lifestyle if we were going to create a meaningful ministry for its members.

For example, in Euclid, we typically planned a big Sunday evening youth event. But in Hutchison, that was family night in the community. So no one came to the Sunday night events. That's why we soon scheduled our youth events on Wednesday nights, because that was church night in the community. Families were important to these people, and that made Hutchison a great place for Jennifer and I to grow our own family.

In partnership with Vern Aruich, the senior pastor, we developed a family-oriented confirmation program to fit the community. I took that with me to my new youth and education position at Concordia Lutheran Church in a suburb of St. Louis, Missouri. I've been there thirteen years.

When we came to Concordia, we started our ministry by meeting with all of the families. We asked them to share their hopes, dreams, and sorrows about teenagers. We kept a record of their responses and based our new ministry on them.

Then we shared with families our hopes for the church's youth ministry—drawn from experiences at our two previous churches. We told them we didn't believe we could do youth ministry at Concordia without parents being involved.

Their hopes and dreams revolved around being involved with their kids. So they responded by helping out—they didn't want to be left out of their kids' faith development at church. They signed up to help with trips, fund-raisers, special events, and outreaches. Our volunteer core was made up of parents, not just unrelated adults. The kids loved it, and that reinforced their parents' decision to get involved. Soon, we had no problem convincing parents to participate in servant projects with kids. In fact, we had to turn some of them away!

In retrospect, our chief goal was to get parents involved with what the church was doing for their kids. We were reaching out to include parents in shaping their kids' faith lives. Today, this is what most consider effective youth ministry, even "family ministry." I hadn't yet taken the next philosophical step—a church that works to get involved in what parents are doing for their kids at home. Our parent plug-in strategy worked then, but many of today's parents rebel against hyperinvolvement in the church. They're refocusing on their homes, and they don't appreciate the church pulling them away from where they want to be. Christian educators are forced to find a new vision.

Denominational leaders asked me to write about the role of parents in youth ministry as part of a thirteen-week leadership training course called "Lead On." In my segment, I compared a youth ministry without parent participation to a tent with a missing pole—it's just a matter of time before the thing collapses. It was a blow to me when my denomination's youth office rejected my vision. "That won't work," they said, "because kids don't want their parents around at youth group." They wanted to tweak my material to limit parent's involvement to what I considered shallow responsibilities— taxi drivers, cooks, and cash machines.

Just after this disappointing news, I was asked to teach a workshop for Christian educators at a conference in Chicago. Still stinging from the brick wall I'd run into, I decided to present my vision at the conference and see how the people responded to it. I came up with five questions that focused on parents' role in youth ministry:

1. Is the parent the single most important factor in the development of an effective person?

2. Were my parents the single most important factor in my development?

3. Are parents of children and teenagers in most churches the single most important factor in their spiritual development?

4. Is it vital to the church's ministry that we support parents?

5. Are parents in the church the primary youth ministers?

Of course, my answer to all five questions was "yes!"

Those Christian educators believed what I was saying, but they didn't know how to translate the philosophy into practical programs.

That spurred me to put something on paper. I came up with a written philosophy for parent participation in confirmation that I developed into a program called "Confirmation: A Family Time." It started as a parent workshop—a preconfirmation meeting for parents to convince them of their important role in their kids' confirmation process.

The parents were thirsting for something their kids liked—something new and different from the lecture approach. And they wanted something they could get involved in. The program included Teen Nights that focused on fellowship that had a ministry purpose, service opportunities, and trips—all planned by families as part of the confirmation program.

I also took "Changes and Choices," our denomination's sex-education curriculum for teenagers, and adapted it into a parent training seminar to help parents grow more comfortable sharing God's plan for sexuality with their kids. I asked parents to teach it to their kids, but if they wouldn't, I told them I would.

Then we planned a New Testament Passover banquet, at which families retold the stories of their kids' births and lives leading up to their confirmation. We had parent meetings that focused on adolescent development and asked families to sign up for early Communion classes together.

The real goal of the program was to create a need in parents to be a part of the ministry. That need was so apparent to us because of our history—when we left Shore Haven, our ministry there died; but when we left Our Redeemer, the ministry continued. Researcher George Barna says, "Most [churchgoing] teens admit that the chances of their leaving the church [after graduation] are at least as good as the chances of staying."[2] That's a tragedy and an indictment of how we're impacting kids.

The point is, if parents aren't integrated into kids' faith development, it's a miracle if their young people continue in the life of the church after confirmation.

I've heard many youth ministers say that their parents just don't support their ministry. But if you structure your ministry to include parents, they will be there. Logos is a Presbyterian midweek program for children through high-school age that is structured to include parents. The Logos system focuses on relationships with parents and other adults as the models for faith development. It's built on an intergenerational structure that clearly communicates that the people listed in the church directory are the real Christian educators in the church. This program is so successful that it's spread throughout the United States and the world. In fact, the Russian Greek Orthodox church has just invited Logos to partner with it in teaching the faith to Russian young people.

About seven years ago, our church welcomed a new senior pastor, Vernon Gundermann. While I was chatting with him at an introductory party, he explained his vision for family ministry. He believed we needed to do fewer ministry activities at church and more at home. He wanted us to open up space in families' lives to give them more time for home activities.

Later, Vern said, "You'll never figure this out unless you go on sabbatical." Because of the paranoia that accompanied my burnout, I thought he was trying to get rid of me. But he honestly thought I was well-equipped to develop church programming that was focused on the home as the primary agency for faith formation.

So on my sabbatical planning retreat with Les Stroh, we hammered out a ministry theory that I could test, a plan for taking over my work, what I would do on the sabbatical, and a schedule for those activities. I brought a pile of research that I thought would help me in developing my plan. One of those resources was a Search Institute study on effective faith development in the church.

According to the people at Search Institute, for a congregation in today's world to be effective in teaching the faith, it must have in place the following essential ministry components:
- a congregational sense of family;
- strong, life-shaping families;
- goal-oriented Christian education; and
- a Christian youth subculture.[3]

I translated these four components into program priorities that made practical sense to me:
- a child-, youth-, and family-friendly church;
- a parent-empowerment system;
- a strong educational ministry for children and youth; and
- a dynamic youth ministry.

The more I thought about these criteria, I wondered how they spoke to parents as primary nurturers of faith in young people. So I developed a working philosophy for passing on the faith from generation to generation. This is it:

"Parents are the primary Christian educators in the church, and the family is the God-ordained institution for faith-building in children and youth and for the passing of faith from one generation to the next."

If this was true, I wanted to discover what the church needs to model in its structure and programming to assist parents and families in that role and task.

Together, Les and I targeted critical issues in my life, my family, and in the life of the church. I planned to use my home to explore how I was nurturing faith in my family and to bring healing to damaged relationships with my wife and daughters. I planned to take time to rest and refresh my mind, spirit, and body. And I determined to test my working philosophy at churches and institutions around the country—across the denominational spectrum—that were pursuing a family-centered philosophy of ministry.[4]

In the sabbatical plan, we thought it was critical to target:

1. **Family Relationships**—The goal was to strengthen family relationships.

2. **New Professional Relationships in Family Ministry**—The goal was to identify six people who I'd be in contact with over the next two years to explore family ministry issues and models.

3. **Rethinking Old Patterns**—The goal was to revisit familiar ministry patterns and explore new approaches.

4. **Researching Strong Families**—The goal was to gather new information and insights to help parents build stronger families.

5. **Refreshment**—The goal was to take time to rest and relax my mind, spirit, and body.

6. **Family Ministry Resources**—The goal was to find fifty to 100 resources to enhance my church's ministry with parents and their families.

7. **Retraining for New Skills**—The goal was to discover options for a course of study for a master's degree in the area of family life.

To gather information to meet the goals for these target areas, we brainstormed four questions to ask at every church and organization I visited:

1. What skills do family members who are making a difference in each other's lives possess?

2. What common values do they share? What do they work to honor and uphold?

3. What's the significant difference that a healthy home makes in the lives of its members? What makes the home the preferred place to invest one's life in?

4. What joys do they celebrate? (If family members are happy, they will cherish the moments they celebrate together.)

We were confident these questions would unlock a treasure chest of family ministry stories and strategies. I presented the plan to church leaders, they approved it, and we put an announcement about my sabbatical in our church newspaper. I also sent a letter to every church family explaining what I hoped to accomplish during my time away. I arranged for interim helpers to cover my responsibilities while I was gone. On my last Sunday, Vern announced from the pulpit that I was on sabbatical, and he strongly encouraged people not to contact me.

The following Monday, I felt scared, excited, relieved, and even confused about what to do next. I had a midmorning breakfast with Les Stroh planned. I showed up unshaven, wearing a T-shirt and shorts. To my surprise, Les said, "That seems very appropriate for a man on sabbatical."

I was on my way, and I could not imagine what God intended for those three months.

I quickly discovered that nothing in my past compared to this style of learning. I was drinking in ideas from people who were in the middle of their passion, and they were thrilled to share with me their perspectives, their strategies, and their hearts. No one I contacted, no matter how well-known he or she was, turned me down. I've always been able to take in a lot of information without bogging down, but I started to feel overwhelmed with the sheer number of great things people were doing to nurture faith in young people by strengthening families.

I crisscrossed the country, visiting five major family-friendly institutions, more than twenty churches, and dozens of church and family professionals. I gleaned from stacks of books, videos, and audiotapes on family issues. I also spent significant time with my family at home, trying to live out what I was learning.

Finally, three months later, after a weekend retreat with Jennifer at a bed-and-breakfast, I walked back into the church on a Monday morning. I was refreshed, relaxed, and bursting to tell people what I'd discovered. I'd planned to share my findings on four consecutive Sunday mornings—to give the most people an opportunity to hear what I had to say, I presented the same information each time. Those presentations formed the seed of this book.

While I was on the road, Dr. Merton Strommen, author of the benchmark book on ministering to young people, *Five Cries of Youth,* told me, "Ben, you have to create a vacuum for change. You have to create in the hearts of people a desire to change so that they'll fill the vacuum with the needed change."

So my hope was not just to share what I'd learned but to create a vacuum that would motivate people to change the way we nurture faith in our families. In my travels, I'd collected the answers to the four questions I'd created. As I shared these answers on those Sunday mornings, an alarm seemed to go off in the people of my church. Why? Because it was apparent that healthy, growing, faith-nurturing families are far more the exception than the rule. I told them what I'd discovered when I asked the "Four Questions":

1. Families that are making a difference in each other's lives possess the following skills:
- teaching the faith;
- nurturing children (especially by fathers);
- empowering others to use their gifts;
- living out the gospel in everyday life;
- setting personal boundaries;
- practicing effective discipline;
- fostering quality interpersonal relationships (family, couple, and friends);
- practicing good family management and planning (finances, time, and decision-making);
- demonstrating the ability to play with children of all ages;
- mentoring;
- showing the ability to teach life skills (lawn care, cleaning, washing, cooking, car maintenance, and balancing a checkbook); and
- fostering interpersonal communication.

2. Families that are making a difference in each other's lives uphold similar values and are working to provide the following:
- a positive learning environment,
- an emphasis on building Christian character,
- lifelong relationships,
- a support system,
- personal identity,
- a sense of belonging, and
- opportunities for faith growth.

3. Families that are making a difference in each other's lives sense that what they're doing—investing their lives in the home—is significant. They feel the following are important products of their homes:
- good marriages that fuel strong families,
- values that reflect God's wisdom,
- people of integrity,
- role models in the faith,
- faith-filled young people,

- family traditions and rituals,
- children who turn into productive adults,
- servant hearts,
- life skills,
- concern for the world outside the home,
- empowerment of people to be the best they can be, and
- support systems for people in crisis.

4. Families that are making a difference in each other's lives joyfully celebrate the following:

- transitions or milestones—from one grade to another, from one job to another, first steps, and so on;
- the gift of life—birthdays, deaths, healings, gardens, and so on;
- children and adults caring for each other—visiting Grandma in the nursing home, helping people who are sick, and so on;
- doing the right thing—resisting vices, choosing to have the baby, forgiving an enemy, deciding not to cheat, and so on;
- achievements—getting a C in a hard class, promotions, an award for artistic excellence, employee of the week, and so on;
- being with each other—choosing to go to the symphony with your parents, choosing to spend recreation time with your family, and so on;
- promises kept—marriage, appointments, commitments, and so on; and
- times faith shows itself—spontaneous prayer, facing fears, loving the unlovable, forgiving the unforgivable, and so on.

This is what family-focused professionals around the country said productive, caring, faith-nurturing families look like—do these lists describe most families in your church and neighborhood?

Rest Stop

Go back through the list of answers under the "Four Questions," and mark a check by each item the majority of your church's or neighborhood's families possess. Circle those items that most of those families need to work on.

After you do this, answer this question: What conclusions can you draw about the homes in your church and neighborhood and the way faith is nurtured in them?_____

_____
_____
_____
_____

It would be rare for any one home to exhibit all these characteristics. But the more of these characteristics a particular home has, the more healthy, vibrant, and fertile that home will be for the nurturing of its family members and their faith.

The truth is, the vast majority of homes do not exhibit a majority of these components. I've worked through this material with more than 3,000 church professionals, and, with few exceptions, they agreed these characteristics describe healthy homes. But these professionals were alarmed at the few characteristics the majority of homes actually exhibit. I asked them to draw "conclusions about typical homes" in their churches and neighborhoods, and they said things such as:

● Family relationships are often strained and disconnected;

● Many families are so much in debt that their activities and relationships are strained;

● Parents struggle to know how to discipline their kids;

● Homes are often not supportive, and are often not fun places to be;

● When parents celebrate their anniversary, some never get a card from their children;

● The pace and volume of family life squeezes out family traditions and activities;

● Families are like puppets controlled by the schedules and priorities of churches, schools, and recreational organizations;

● The media coming into many homes is rarely, if ever, monitored; and

● Many homes are more like rest stops than places to belong and grow.

The people who came to these conclusions weren't bashing families; they were simply alarmed at what they now realized. Most said they'd assumed—wrongly—that they understood the culture of the home. Consequently, they were blind to many of its needs, struggles, and wounds. Home life has changed right under our noses, but it has happened so gradually, so subtly, that it's evaded detection. Or, more accurately, we were mesmerized into inactivity by these changes.

Typically, parents receive the bulk of the blame for all this. In a 1997 Public Agenda survey, only one in five adults said it's "very common" to find parents who are good role models. Half said parents spoil their kids or fail to discipline them. And more than half (56 percent) of the women surveyed said today's mothers are worse than their own mothers.[5] But the facts make it clear that parents have been made scapegoats for widespread problems in the home. The truth is…

● Mothers today are more likely to attend their children's school events than their own mothers were;

● Parents today spend just as much time with their kids as '60s parents did;

• Because today's families are smaller, each child receives more parental attention;

• Families today are more likely than '70s families to do a wide variety of activities together.[6]

The unseen enemy of stable homes is a culture of disunity that can't agree on what's right and wrong for kids. According to writer Cheryl Russell in American Demographics, "Parents of the 1950s could afford to be laissez-faire about child-rearing. The schools, the media, the neighbors—all worked together to ensure the success of their offspring. Parents of the 1990s know only too well the danger lurking behind a stranger's smile, the undertow of failure awaiting children whose parents are not vigilant."[7]

So parents are, in some ways, working harder than ever to raise their kids well. But they're fighting an uphill battle. During my presentations, I could see light bulbs going off in these church professionals' heads—it's the culture itself that's in opposition to faith-nurturing, strong families. And the church is stuck in an old pattern of teaching the faith to families—its programming and structure is focused to meet the needs of families in a culture that does not exist anymore.

For example: Sunday schools that pattern themselves after 1950s-era educational models; youth ministries that still follow a stand-alone "minichurch" model that discourages church-wide involvement; church programs that segregate age levels almost exclusively and require families to separate to participate in church activities; and faith-development strategies that assume, wrongly, that homes are partnering with the church to teach kids about Jesus.

It breaks my heart that we haven't challenged families to make Christ a higher priority in their day-to-day lives. We've simply rubber-stamped families' decision to let the church teach their children the faith. We've been lulled into perpetuating destructive patterns, and we have even championed those patterns by the way we've structured our churches.

Rest Stop

Put a check mark next to each "conclusion about typical homes" on page 26 that are true of your own family or your family of origin. Circle the conclusions that are true of families in your church.

Now list the top three destructive patterns emerging in your church's families:

1_____

2_____

3_____

Is your church enabling these patterns or opposing them?

Clearly, the church needs a philosophical overhaul. In my twenty-five years of ministry, I worked very hard at developing a *church-centered* youth- and children's-ministry. I said to families, "Bring your kids to me. Let me teach them the faith, and I'll involve you in the process. Help me develop good Sunday schools, a great vacation Bible school, a midweek program, servant events, retreats, evangelism trips, youth-oriented worship," and on and on.

The message I was communicating to families was that the church should be the focal point for nurturing faith in their kids. *I wanted families to invest their energy in what the church was about rather than the church investing its energy in what families are about.* I was sucking the life out of families for the sake of the church's mission.

But I'd missed the point. I, too, had been drawn into the program-centered culture. When Jennifer and I die and we're standing before Christ, he's not going to ask our pastor or our youth minister, "How did you nurture the faith of Cori and Sara?" He's going to ask *us* because we, not the church, are responsible for helping our daughters grow in faith. On the other hand, he *will* ask the church, "How did you support Ben and Jennifer in the nurture of faith in their home?"

But before we can explore what a home-centered, church-supported style will look like in the church, we must first evaluate what we're doing in our own homes to nurture faith. If we don't, everything we do to help transform the church will ring false.

You already know what was going on in my home. When I decided to take my three-month sabbatical, I intended to use my home and family as the experiential base to discover how to live a balanced life and to grow more home-centered. But the prospect of Dad at home every night for three months was scarier for Jennifer and the girls than it was for me. You see, I didn't have any idea what I was getting into...but they did.

> That's why I'm convinced we must shift from a church-centered, home-supported ministry model to a home-centered, church-supported ministry model. I now believe that parents are the primary Christian educators in the church and the family is the God-ordained institution for faith-building in children and youth and for passing the faith on from one generation to the next.

Notes

[1] Peter L. Benson, Ph.D.; Eugene C. Roehlkepartain; and I. Shelby Andress, *Congregations at Crossroads: A National Study of Adults and Youth in the Lutheran Church—Missouri Synod* (Minneapolis, MN: Search Institute, 1995), 21.

[2] George Barna, *Generation Next* (Ventura, CA: Regal Books, 1995), 92.

[3] Dr. Dale Blyth, *Healthy Communities; Healthy Youth,* a study funded by RespecTeen (Minneapolis, MN: Search Institute, 1991).

[4] I conducted formal interviews with more than fifty family ministry practitioners and experts across the country, including visits with Dr. Merton Strommen, author of *Five Cries of Youth;* Eugene C. Roehlkepartain of Search Institute; Roger Charman of Focus on the Family; Rollie Martinson of Luther Seminary; Dr. John Westerhoff, author of *Will Our Children Have Faith*; and dozens of practitioners in innovative churches.

[5] Cheryl Russell, "What's Wrong With Kids?" (citing statistics from a 1997 survey by Public Agenda) (American Demographics, November 1997), 12.

[6] Russell, "What's Wrong With Kids?", 14-15.

[7] Ibid., 15.

Section 2
Five Discoveries About the Home

Maintaining your balance in life is hard work, but it's even more difficult to be home-centered when you work for a volunteer-based organization such as the church. Why?

1. Much of church work happens on weekends and evenings. The very hours we're expected to be at work are the hours our families are at home. Therefore, we have to come up with creative ways to be with them. And that takes discipline—all the time, everywhere.

2. People in the church really want us to take time off, unless, of course, they need us for *their* crisis or *their* project. Because we're dealing with many projects at one time, we're always working on somebody's top priority. We're beholden to many bosses.

3. It's hard to expect more from a volunteer than you expect from yourself. If I have a weekend retreat with a group of young people and my adult leaders have to go to work on Monday, what right do I have to take Monday off?

4. Sacrifice is a part of servant living—and we're expected to be model servants of Christ. We often confuse sacrifice with martyrdom—the need to be somebody's savior. So when I have a date with my wife and a "crisis" comes up, I sacrifice what I most value for what could have waited until tomorrow—because, in a twisted way, it seems Christlike.

The church is a mission-based organization, and we know our "company slogan" all too well: "A good shepherd lays down his life for the sheep." But you know what? You've got to *have a life* before you can lay it down when you need to. So many of us have interpreted "lay down your life" as "obliterate your boundaries." That's not what Jesus meant, and in this section, we'll explore the difference between a life of Christlike service and a boundary-less life.

I spent three months focusing on the ways I'd been unbalanced in my home life. During that time, I learned five crucial truths. They've completely transformed my thinking about who I want to be at home—as husband, as father, and as Ben.

I can't stress strongly enough that we must be working to transform our own homes before we can transform our church's ministry to a family-friendly philosophy. It's hard to be a catalyst for home-centered ministry when your own home life is a poor model. That's why self-examination in this section is critical. Believe me, I know it's not easy to shine a light on the places in our lives we'd prefer to keep in the shadows. But it's liberating to do it. I found that out...the hard way.

Chapter 3
Family Business

I couldn't think about changing the church until I thought about changing my own relationship to my family and my home. I'd always focused on chores and family relationships with "leftover time." I believed that paying bills, cutting grass, painting, and completing other household tasks were not really a part of my work. So I did family things in crisis mode—I paid bills the night before they were due, I cut the grass only because it was six inches high and company was coming over, and I fit in my bathroom-cleaning chore at midnight.

If you think about it, I was living the life of a modern Gnostic—only the "spiritual" things in life were important enough to invest my quality time in. I fundamentally looked down my nose at the tasks required for living in a physical world.

Today my approach to these responsibilities is totally different. I now believe that...

Managing the "family business" is the most important work that needs to be done, and my calendar must reflect this priority.

While on sabbatical, I read books about bringing my life into balance, I listened to tapes on adrenalin addiction, and I asked almost everyone I interviewed how they managed their lives. When these resources painted a picture of burnout, they described me. And when the leaders I interviewed talked about their own imbalanced lives, they revealed hurtful patterns in me that I'd never suspected.

As I came to grips with who I'd become, I was determined to change. Jennifer described me as a workaholic whose mistress was church work, but part of me refused to believe it. Suddenly, it was so clear to me...she was absolutely right. This revelation humbled me and made me desperate for a way out of the spiral.

On my way home from an appointment in Tennessee, I was listening in my car to tapes that promised to help me balance my life. I noticed a self-help pamphlet in the cassette-tape box. I was so hungry for help, I tried to read it while I was driving. But I couldn't do it. So I stopped at a McDonald's and read through the whole thing, marking ideas like my life depended on it.

I felt as though I'd been happily adrift in a rowboat headed swiftly toward a chasm, and for years I'd worked as hard as I could pulling on the oars, blind to my path while proud of my effort. Now, perched on the precipice, I'd sneaked a peek behind me. I quickly, frantically realized I'd have to turn my boat around now or risk heading over the edge. I was cranking hard on those oars and inching my way back upstream.

I prayed a lot during this time. I begged my Father to forgive me for what I'd done to my family and to myself. I asked him to give me direction in repairing my damaged relationships. Out of this stew of desperate seeking and desperate prayer came a deep desire to be at home. To *be* at home. And I had three months to live out my desire.

As the months progressed, I noticed myself...

- cutting the grass regularly—I took every Friday afternoon off just to get it done;
- taking time in the morning to pay bills, before I started work;
- going grocery shopping with the whole family—making it a relationship-building experience;
- planning work days and assigning responsibilities to tackle big home-maintenance tasks such as painting three rooms in our home; and
- setting aside time with Jennifer each week to plan our family schedule—so the family stuff got on the calendar first.

During this time, I realized the skills I use at church to plan and organize my ministry are skills I can transfer to the home. For example, I recommend developing:

- **A family mission statement***—Most churches work hard at crafting a statement of purpose, but few of us take the time to write down the reason our family exists. Ours says: "Our home is a safe place of shelter from the storms of life. It equips our family members to positively impact our home, neighborhood, community, and world through the gifts God's given them."

- **A family financial plan**—As church workers, we know we must prudently and wisely use the gifts people have given the church. To do that, we typically put in place a sophisticated financial-management system that ensures integrity and accountability in all money matters. We can apply the same stewardship principles to our family finances. Every year, we visit with a family financial planner who helps us plan for the future and avoid unnecessary debt.

- **A plan for family goals and activities**—As a church-staff leader, I'm required to lead our youth, education, and family ministry board members through a planning process that helps them identify critical targets, set goals, and plan activities. If you use a similar planning process at home, you'll bring significance to your family's activities because you'll be focused on what's most important to everyone. For example, Jennifer and I have developed a list

*For guidance in developing your own family mission statement, see the Appendix on page 144.

of fourteen hopes* for our children's futures—the list helps us make good decisions about the activities they get involved in.

● **A family schedule**—At most churches, a staffer is responsible for the master calendar. It helps the church stay organized and prevents the church from overscheduling its time and facilities. At home, we have a master activity-calendar that offers the same safeguards to our family. We let our girls know they can't expect us to change our schedule if they ask us to make the change on the day of the activity.

● **A time-management system**—In the church, we use sophisticated, often expensive, time-management systems to organize our most precious resource—time. At home, we need ways to make the best use of our time and keep peace in the family. In my day planner, I have a section reserved for home activities and responsibilities. Some time-management companies have caught on to this emerging family need. Day-Timer is trumpeting on its newest catalog cover a computer tool to "balance your family life." Called "Day-Timer HomeLife," it features coordinated family schedules, prioritized to-do lists, a "Leave Messages on the Fridge" electronic bulletin board, and other ideas.

I know these ideas can seem overwhelming if you think you have to do them all at once. So pace yourself—start by trying one. You're probably doing something in each area already and just need to be more deliberate about your plans.

Rest Stop

Since managing the "family business" is the most important work that needs to be done and your calendar must reflect this priority…

● Look at your calendar. Is your family and home the most important work in your life?___Yes___No

● What are three items on last month's calendar that indicate the value you place on your home or family?

1.

2.

3.

● Are there changes that need to be made? If so, list some.

*For a diagram that lists these hopes, see the Appendix on page 147.

Quiet Detour

It's time to reconnect with God through word and prayer. The Quiet Detours you encounter in this section look remarkably similar to each other, but they have subtle differences in focus. The similarities emphasize key issues affecting all homes. The differences highlight the changing needs of *your* home. Enjoy this ritual approach to prayer; let it open new communication patterns with God.

What I need: Help in giving my home and family a high priority in my life.

"But for Adam no suitable helper was found. So the Lord God caused the man to fall into a deep sleep; and while he was sleeping, he took one of the man's ribs and closed up the place with flesh. Then the Lord God made a woman from the rib he had taken out of the man, and he brought her to the man. The man said, 'This is now bone of my bones and flesh of my flesh; she shall be called "woman," for she was taken out of man.' For this reason a man will leave his father and mother and be united to his wife, and they will become one flesh. The man and his wife were both naked, and they felt no shame" (Genesis 2:20b-25).

Dear Father in heaven,

Thank you for the gifts of family and home. Grant me the wisdom to honor these gifts by being a good steward of them. Protect those who live in my home, that the wicked foe may have no power over them. Give me the courage to shape and nurture my home according to your will, giving time and energy to shape it into a place where your grace and love abound. May it become a place where your Word is learned and lived. Help me see the important role my home plays in the lives of those who live there, and teach me to care for it with all of my power and strength. Guide me in this journey, and open me to your will.

Amen.

Chapter 4
Quantity and Quality

When my oldest daughter, Cori, was very young, she called me "Bye-bye." That stuck with me for a long time. She thought I was Bye-bye, not Daddy. By the time I was at Concordia in St. Louis, I had a loving relationship with my daughters, but Cori always sensed she took second place to other people and other commitments.

As I think about it now, I'm saddened by the time I've lost—forever—with my oldest daughter. And that time translates into memories I'll never have.

I'm grateful I was given the time and grace to start over. During the sabbatical, when I was not traveling, I was at home. I mean, *really* at home. My relationship with my daughters grew by leaps and bounds. I was with my family in the evenings—not at meetings or in the office. I was just there. I deliberately didn't do anything. I just sat there and watched. It was great.

As time passed, my daughters started to trust that I'd be there for them. They began sharing about their days at school. Questions popped up about conflicts with friends and school assignments. I remember Cori asking me about the role of women in the church for a writing assignment. They even asked me for tips on using our computer. We didn't just discuss answers to their problems; we began sharing our feelings.

I asked Sara if I could join her in practicing her basketball skills, and she was thrilled. I made appointments with my daughters to take them each to breakfast for time alone with Dad. I went with an agenda and an arsenal of questions—I so much wanted them to know I cared about them and their lives. So I pressed a little. Instead of conversation, I got dead silence. This was harder than I thought.

They just wanted to eat and talk and do what people in "normal" families do: relax with each other. Cori told me, "Dad, this isn't a youth group 'Coke Date'—this is just eating breakfast like a family!" To this day, I'm still learning the difference between my roles as Dad and as youth minister.

I began to transfer my knowledge, understanding, skills, values, and faith in real ways—on their turf, on their time schedule. I've often heard that quality time is more important than quantity time. But I don't buy it anymore—both quality time and quantity time are important. In fact, Newsweek made the decades-old debate over quality time vs. quantity time its cover article for a May 1997 issue. In it, Harvard psychologist Ronald Levant says, "I think quality time is just a way of deluding ourselves into shortchanging our children.

Children need vast amounts of parental time and attention. It's an illusion to think they're going to be on your timetable, and that you can say, 'OK, we've got a half hour, let's get on with it.' "[1]

The truth is...

If we are to nurture faith in our children, if we are to pass on our values and wisdom, we must be willing to spend a quantity of time in a quality way.

It's often during quantity time that quality time emerges. I'd always believed that attending my daughters' school activities—volleyball matches, basketball games, track meets, and plays—was a good catalyst for relationship. It *is* important to be at their activities. But relationships require more than just watching; you must have contact—eye to eye, mouth-to-ear, mind-to-mind, and heart-to-heart.

In the groundbreaking book *The Time Bind: When Work Becomes Home & Home Becomes Work,* author Arlie Russell Hochschild says our intense commitment to work is siphoning away the time and energy we need to invest in our families. And children are the big losers—more and more, Hochschild says, they don't get the time they need with a fully engaged, fully alert parent.[2]

In her review of the book in Fast Company magazine, working single mom Candice Carpenter describes a retreat she and her business partner took to take stock of their work-life commitments. She says, "There are 168 hours in a seven-day week. The time needed to complete our list of activities exceeded 230 hours. While we could accomplish a burst of work in an all-nighter, we couldn't cram raising our children into compressed shifts. Instead I've decided that I owe my daughter what I call 'lazy time': wandering, unscheduled, lolling time, with my full attention."

Carpenter sums up the impact of *The Time Bind* on her life by asking herself an important question: "What if we apply the same creativity, energy, and engagement to our pursuit of 'home' as we do to our pursuit of work? I'm ready to do the time."[3]

Why is this quantity-and-quality issue so important? Because relationships are the key to understanding, to trust, to conflict resolution, to forgiveness, and to God's imperatives—love him, and our neighbors, as ourselves. Relationships lead to lifelong joys—shared and celebrated.

Slowly, I've added quantity time to quality time with my family...

● Cori and I took our first camping trip together her first summer after college—to the Land Between the Lakes in Kentucky.

● Our family and two of the girls' friends went to "Grandma's cabin" (Jennifer's mother owns it) to relax and be family. I left my agendas at home.

● Jennifer and I went to visit Cori in the Dominican Republic during her semester of studying abroad. We didn't go primarily to sightsee but to be a part of her experience. We wanted to make a memory with her. When she decided to go, we realized she would return after the experience excited about all she learned and saw. We wanted to be connected to this very significant phase of her life.

● When Sara was struggling to decide whether to stay at her college or transfer to another one, she called us for advice on balancing her checkbook. We realized we'd never taught her this important life skill. So instead of working through it on the phone, we decided to get in the car and do it face to face. It's a four-hour drive, so we left on a Friday afternoon and came back Saturday night so we could fulfill our duties at church. It was probably the best thing we ever did. It sent a clear message that we supported and loved her in the midst of her freshman struggles. In that quantity of time, the quality emerged.

● On Cori's twenty-first birthday, she was at a summer job in Michigan. We decided we didn't want to miss this milestone. So Jennifer, Sara, and I drove eight hours to Holland, Michigan just to celebrate and say, "Happy birthday!" Four years ago, my priorities would've overshadowed and ultimately dismissed a trip like this.

I've learned that if I want to pass on my faith, values, wisdom, and knowledge—and have my kids absorb them—I must spend time building relationships with my kids. They won't just "catch" these things haphazardly. We must be deliberate—just as I'm deliberate in my relationships with kids in the youth group. When we do, our kids will catch what we throw their way. For example…

1. **Celebrate achievements, large and small.** Give daisies for a report well-done, buy a favorite treat and put it in a child's room with a note, buy baseball tickets as an after-SAT test surprise, or write a personal note and tape it to a bathroom mirror.

2. **Celebrate birthdays in unique ways.** Take a special surprise in a gift bag tied with a bow to school, and give it to your child in front of his or her friends.

3. **Write poems to mark special times together.** Most people think they're not talented enough to write a poem, but that's not true. It's a lot easier than you think. If you're stuck, take a simple nursery rhyme and change the words.

4. **Offer to help your kids with their chores, or create special projects.** Plant a garden and name it together, help wash the car they use, cook a meal and invite some of their friends to eat it with you, or create a scrapbook album that focuses on a special interest.

5. **Go on picnics together.** Brainstorm unique places around your area (one of our special picnic places was near a fountain by a bank) and then work together to prepare a "favorites" meal and eat it at one of the places.

6. **Play like kids.** Go fly a kite, blow bubbles, make paper airplanes, play jacks, discover the wonder of a yo-yo, toss the Frisbee around. The only hard and fast rule is...have fun!

As *The Time Bind* points out, so many kids in our culture don't get what they want most—their parents' time. In place of that precious resource, kids often get a hollow substitute—money or stuff. When we recognize the real treasure kids covet and give it to them, it'll make a drastic change in how we relate to each other. I've spent twenty-five years listening to the core concerns of teenagers, and I believe if parents understood this one truth, many of the negative behaviors kids exhibit would dwindle.

Rest Stop

Since we must be willing to spend a quantity of time in a quality way if we're to nurture faith in our children and pass on our values...

● What plans do you have to be with your children next week (or if you're single or without children, with your parents, siblings, or close friends)?

● Are there changes you need to make in your schedule? If so, list them.

Quiet Detour

It's time again to reconnect with God through word and prayer.

What I need: Time to pass on the faith to the next generation.

"There is a time for everything, and a season for every activity under heaven: a time to be born and a time to die, a time to plant and a time to uproot, a time to kill and a time to heal, a time to tear down and a time to build, a time to weep and a time to laugh, a time to mourn and a time to dance, a time to scatter stones and a time to gather them, a time to embrace and a time to refrain, a time to search and a time to give up, a time to keep and a time to throw away, a time to tear and a time to mend, a time to be silent and a time to speak, a time to love and a time to hate, a time for war and a time for peace.

What does the worker gain from his toil? I have seen the burden God has laid on men. He has made everything beautiful in its time. He has also set eternity in the hearts of men; yet they cannot fathom what God has done from beginning to end. I know that there is nothing better for men than to be happy and do good while they live. That everyone may eat and drink, and find satisfaction in all his toil—this is the gift of God. I know that everything God does will endure forever; nothing can be added to it and nothing taken from it. God does it so that men will revere him. Whatever is has already been, and what will be has been before; and God will call the past to account (Ecclesiastes 3:1-15).

Dear Father in heaven,

Thank you for the gifts of family, home, and time. Grant me the wisdom to honor these gifts by being a good steward of them. Protect those who live in my home, that the wicked foe may have no power over them. Give me the courage to shape and nurture my home according to your will, giving time and energy to shape it into a place where your grace and love abound. May it become a place where your Word is learned and lived. Help me to use the time you give me to affirm those who live in my home as special people of God who are so valuable that I would use the gift of time to care for, love, and teach them your ways. Guide me in this journey, and open me to your will.

Amen.

Notes

[1] Laura Shapiro, "The Myth of Quality Time," Newsweek (May 12, 1997), 64.

[2] Arlie Russell Hochschild, *The Time Bind: When Work Becomes Home & Home Becomes Work* (Metropolitan Books, 1997).

[3] Candice Carpenter, "Working on Borrowed Time," Fast Company (August/September 1997), 68.

Chapter 5
Nothing's "Natural" About Healthy Relationships

I've realized how strong love is. If our love for each other had not been strong, how could our marriage have survived? Jennifer and I used to go to high school athletic events to watch our kids and youth group members play. Once inside the gym, I'd leave Jennifer sitting alone on a bleacher and do a little PR work among church members. Jennifer felt consistently abandoned.

I'm a hugger. So when we went to church functions, I typically paid more attention to teenagers, teammates, and adult volunteers than Jennifer. I went into megahug mode, embracing everyone but my wife. After twenty years of this subtle rejection, she saw my attention to others as "hugging the mistress."

We'd often arrive at church social-functions together. But soon after, I'd wander off to talk to people—answering questions, listening to struggles, being supportive. In Jennifer's eyes, there was nothing wrong with connecting with people, but why couldn't I involve her in what I was doing? I'd left her for "a better date."

On evenings when I was off doing church work, people would call our home and Jennifer would assume the role of church secretary—even though our church had a staffer answering the phone until 9:30 every night. After two decades of this subtle invasion of our home, something in my wife would seethe after the fifth call of the night—"How dare the mistress call us at home!"

By the time Jennifer delivered her ultimatum to me about my out-of-control life, my choices had begun to drive a wedge between us. But without our knowledge, God had already started us on a new path. And it came through the very thing that was separating us—my work.

My retired senior pastor and friend, Walter Schoedel, was working with Dr. David Ludwig, a pastor and leader of The Family Initiative (an organization that aims to make our denomination more family-friendly) on a pilot project for nurturing families in the church. They invited me to participate. My job was to bring a group of people from our church to a family-focused retreat where they would evaluate Dr. Ludwig's resource entitled "Renewing the Family Spirit."

At that retreat, Jennifer and I learned things we'd never before understood about each other. Because we were there together, we found common ground to grow through some of our struggles. We saw more clearly how our unique histories and communication styles led to many of our relational meltdowns.

We traced the issues that were causing the "storms" in our relationship. In fact, Ludwig compares relational struggles to storm patterns and tries to teach couples to be better "weather forecasters." Obviously, God created men and women differently, and I didn't understand how to embrace and celebrate Jennifer's differences.

We offered to take Ludwig's materials and make them more accessible for lay people in the church, in the process immersing ourselves all over again in the learning process. Then, during the three months of my sabbatical, Jennifer and I had ample time to practice the skills we'd learned. We cried together, laughed together, and grew together. We prayed and dreamed dreams. We discovered play in our relationship. We...

- planned "Movie Dates After 9:00 p.m.,"
- scheduled "couple planning" breakfasts,
- enjoyed a special "Jennifer's Favorite" snack and movie in bed, and
- spent a weekend together at a bed-and-breakfast and went antique shopping.

Through it all, we relearned an important truth:

Skills in parenting, in being family, and in being a couple are learned skills. No one is simply given a strong spiritual foundation of skills for marriage and family—they must be learned.*

Life-giving relationships rarely grow unattended—they need to be nurtured. That's why weeds seem to grow even when we're trying to kill them, but a lawn could die if not cared for. Good relationships take work and attention. We must...

1. **Learn together**—Go to workshops and marriage retreats to improve your relationship. Read books and listen to tapes on intimacy and relationship skills.

2. **Pray together**—Sounds simple, but it's not easy. When you pray, you open your souls to each other. The better your relationship, the more you'll relax in this vulnerability.

3. **Be together**—Recognize that no matter how long you've been together, there are always new and exciting things to learn about each other. You must always tend your garden, or the weeds will choke out what is beautiful.

---

*According to a study by Franklin Covey Company Research, about half (46 percent) of all Americans wish they'd taken parenting classes before they had kids.[1]

People say the best gift you can give your children is to love your spouse. These words have become real to me. I think I've even accepted them as truth.

Rest Stop

(This rest stop is focused on parents, but married couples without children or single people who are working with children or who hope someday to be married can benefit from thinking about these questions.)

Since skills in parenting, in being family, and in being a couple are learned skills, and no one is simply given a strong spiritual foundation or skills for marriage and family...

● Think about the last parenting course you took—what did you learn?

● If you've never taken a course in parenting skills, where did you learn what you know? What do you wish you knew better?

● Think about a class or retreat you've attended that focused on "couple skills"—what did you learn?

● Think about a book you've read that relates to marriage, parenting, or family—what did you learn?

● Are there changes that need to be made in the way you relate to your spouse and family? If so, list some.

Quiet Detour

It's time again to reconnect with God through word and prayer.

What I need: Knowledge and wisdom to live in healthy relationships with those in my home, especially my spouse.

"Blessed are all who fear the Lord, who walk in his ways. You will eat the fruit of your labor; blessings and prosperity will be yours. Your wife will be like a fruitful vine within your house; your sons will be like olive shoots around your table. Thus is the man blessed who fears the Lord. May the Lord bless you from Zion all the days of your life; may you see the prosperity of Jerusalem, and may you live to see your children's children. Peace be upon Israel" (Psalm 128).

Dear Father in heaven,

Thank you for the gifts of family, home, time and relationship. Grant me the wisdom to honor these gifts by being a good steward of them. Protect those who live in my home, that the wicked foe may have no power over them. Give me the courage to shape and nurture my home according to your will, giving time and energy to shape it into a place where your grace and love abound. May it become a place where your Word is learned and lived. Help me to grow in my knowledge and skills for relating to the people in my home. Teach me to listen, forgive, understand, hear, and be for them what you are to me—my joy and hope. Guide me in this journey, and open me to your will.

Amen.

Notes

[1] from a Business Wire report of the September 1997 results of a Franklin Covey Company Research survey of 600 adults.

Chapter 6
Church vs. Home

A church's structure and programs have surprising power to set family agendas—especially staffers' families. Throughout most of my ministry, I'd always accepted the church's right to dictate my family's schedule. Doesn't that sound ridiculous? But I accepted this arrangement, as do most church workers I know, because I sensed I had a higher calling: I'm on a mission from God. Therefore, like a good soldier, I did what I was told.

For example, this was a typical Christmas Eve schedule for our family:

7:30 a.m.—I arrive at church.

3:30 p.m.—My family arrives at church.

5:00 p.m.—I lead a children's service that always involves my family in the program.

7:00 p.m.—I lead a second children's service—again with help from my family.

8:15 p.m.—We eat peanut butter and jelly (in a good year, ham and cheese) sandwiches in my office.

9:00 p.m.—I assist in our Christmas candlelight service, which my family attends.

11:00 p.m.—I assist in a second candlelight service; my family sticks around to greet people at the beginning and then leaves for home to prepare for our family celebration.

12:30 a.m.—I get home, and we open our gifts. (The next morning, I give a rather elaborate children's message at the 10:00 a.m. Christmas service.)

Sound a little familiar to you?

The question is, how family-friendly is the typical church worker's schedule? It depends on who's controlling the schedule—you or the church. And do most church workers feel as though they even have the option? Likely, you don't. Again, people on a mission are expected, and expect themselves, to give up their lives for the cause.

The point is that the church schedule can help families grow strong or it can hinder their relationships by keeping them from home priorities. I really thought I was being family-sensitive when I involved parents and kids in the planning and programming of the church. If I was inviting parents to participate, I must be family-friendly. That's what "family ministry" is all about, right? Until my three-month epiphany, I had little understanding of how all my planning affected people's homes. And I hadn't embraced *home-centered* family ministry.

For example, we used to schedule three different children's choirs on any given Sunday morning. The problem was, many families had kids in more than one choir, so they had to go to multiple services if they wanted to support their children. We just weren't thinking in a family-focused way. Our programming was having a profoundly negative impact on family life, and we didn't recognize the problem until kids stopped showing up and parents started complaining.

I traditionally scheduled our summer canoe-trip over the Father's Day weekend. One year, when one of my adult volunteers asked, "But it's Father's Day. Is this a good idea?" I responded, "How long do kids need to celebrate Father's Day? Couldn't they celebrate before they leave or when they get back?"

It's not just the church's scheduling—it's a deeper problem. The issue is how the church staff perceives the value of the home as it schedules its programs. Quite literally, Ben the church staffer was killing Ben the husband and father's family time. I was both victim and victimizer. That's a reality not just for me, but for so many church staffers. It wasn't until I slowed my own pace that I could see how the church's hyperdrive schedule was gobbling up the "time buffers" I needed to simply enjoy life with my family.

To help me understand what it was like to enjoy these "time buffers" during the holidays, we planned a family vacation in Arizona over Christmas. For the first time in my life, I sat with my family on Christmas Eve and Christmas Day. I watched my daughters sing and noticed their hearts dance with joy as they worshiped.

We sat in the front row of a big church. There was a manger scene down front. There were long-haired camels in the scene. One of our girls turned to Jennifer and asked, "Mom, is that a rat in the manger scene?" Jennifer looked at it and started giggling. Then her giggles went kind of nuclear—her whole body was shaking. The pew was vibrating. And we all caught a service-long case of the giggles from her. Afterward, I realized we were doing something on Christmas Eve that was rare in our family—we were laughing together and enjoying each other's company. Quite a contrast from our typical, harried Christmas separateness. That night, I thought, "Christmas Eve couldn't get much better than this."

Over Christmas, we had decided to do a family servant-project. I had called the church ahead of time to get the name of a needy family so we could provide a Christmas dinner and gifts for them. We pooled our money, and the friends we were staying with chipped in. We went together to purchase the food, buy the gifts, wrap them, and deliver it all to the family that afternoon. This idea is nothing new for a youth minister—I'd done the same thing with thirty-five teenagers. But now I was doing it with my family.

During the sabbatical, we tried to stay away from our church and, instead, visit other churches in our area. We wanted to know what it would feel like to go to church as a family without being known as a staffer's family. Instead of going to Sunday school, we typically went to a restaurant to debrief the experience. We had great discussions about what we felt, saw, and heard. Our conversations always centered on what we'd learned about our faith through the service. I wondered if Sunday school could be any better than this.

Freed from the tyranny of overwrought ministry expectations, I could focus on what was most important to me—my own family's spiritual growth. That helped me to see…

The church has a significant role in the life and faith of the family; that impact can be bad or good, depending on the church's structure and programming.

You and I have more control than we think in determining whether the church's impact on our families will be positive or negative. For example…

1. Now I often sit with my family in the worship service, even if I'm playing a leadership role. And I think the congregation likes it.

2. I've given myself permission to say "no" to the church's schedule when it conflicts with my family's schedule.

3. We use our answering machine to monitor our calls so the phone doesn't interrupt our schedule.

4. I'm much more sensitive when I schedule programs. I think about each activity's impact on families before I add it in. Sometimes we get great ideas for events, but because of the cost to our families, we decide the pain isn't worth the gain. We're getting better at saying "no" to some of our big ideas, thereby saying "yes" to families.

As professional church workers, maybe it's time we stop thinking of ourselves as victims. We need to stop whining about how much the church dictates our lives and begin to be more responsible for our own families.

So often, Jennifer was angry at the church for using up all my available time because I basically blamed the church for my inability to set boundaries for family time. The truth is, if we're looking for someone to blame, we'd best begin with ourselves. Church consultant (and my friend) Les Stroh says we have three legitimate options in any work situation: (1) accept the situation the way it is and live with it, (2) be deliberate toward effecting change, or (3) move on.

If we choose (1), we're either recognizing that there are some things we just can't change or that it's not a hill we want to die on. So we choose to live with our situation. If we choose (2), we must develop a strategy to effect change and then implement it the best way we can. If we choose (3), we recognize we can't make the needed change and we're not willing to live with the situation the way it is. We've got to move on. But in any case, it's up to us to choose a path for ourselves.

Rest Stop

Since the church's impact on the family can be bad or good depending on the church's structure and programming...

● Does your church, in its program and structure, pull your family apart or often overrule your personal schedule? If you answered "yes," give an example:

● If you answered "no," what is your church doing to help protect your family and personal time?

● Obviously, if your church's impact on your family is more bad than good, you've got choices to make. You might not be able to change your church, but you can change yourself. List three things you can do to protect your boundaries for family time.

Quiet Detour

It's time again to reconnect with God through word and prayer.

What I need: Wisdom, courage, and a gentle spirit in encouraging my church to value the home in the church's program and structure.

"Listen, O heavens, and I will speak; hear, O earth, the words of my mouth. Let my teaching fall like rain and my words descend like dew, like showers on new grass, like abundant rain on tender plants. I will proclaim the name of the Lord. Oh, praise the greatness of our

God! He is the Rock, his works are perfect, and all his ways are just. A faithful God who does no wrong, upright and just is he" (Deuteronomy 32:1-4).

Dear Father in heaven,

Thank you for the gifts of family, home, time, relationships, and my church. Grant me the wisdom to honor these gifts by being a good steward of them. Protect those who live in my home, that the wicked foe may have no power over them. Give me the courage to shape and nurture my home according to your will, giving time and energy to shape it into a place where your grace and love abound. May it become a place where your Word is learned and lived. Help me be like "abundant rain on tender plants," that what I say and do may grow the church in your will and way. Give me the courage to bring change where it's needed. I pray the church would see your vision for the home. Use my home as a model for the church to learn from. Guide me in this journey, and open me to your will.

Amen.

Chapter 7
Regaining Control

For years, I lived by default. That means I did my work and lived my life without deliberately thinking about the relationship between my choices and my family's mission and purpose. So when a project came up at work and I was asked to do it, I'd say "sure" 90 percent of the time. I didn't consider how work projects would impact my life—and especially my family's health and well-being.

Often, our church planned a congregational fall retreat for people of all ages. The lay leaders who'd previously organized the event decided it was time to give others the "opportunity." At that time I was our church's youth minister, so the event was outside my responsibilities. At a church staff meeting, however, my senior pastor asked me to organize the retreat. Of course, I said "yes."

That one seemingly innocent decision allocated two hundred hours of my time—above and beyond my regular workload—to a work project rather than my duties at home. I sacrificed precious time with my family to plan a retreat for other people's families. Can you taste the irony here? What's more, it was a decent retreat, but not well-attended. Its impact was minimal.

A few years ago, a youth worker from another church called to ask if I'd be a presenter at their two-day senior high retreat. The last thing I needed in my life was a two-day commitment at another church. And there were plenty of well-qualified people around who could do what he was asking me to do.

So, of course, I said "yes."

I didn't check to see how this commitment would affect my family's life. It turns out the retreat was scheduled over the same weekend my daughter was playing in an important basketball tournament. I missed the basketball tournament.

Good organizations are, by design, mission-driven and goal-oriented. They're fueled by a deliberate action plan, and the CEO's job is to make sure the organization stays on course.

Without realizing it, families have become a part of the deliberate plans of companies, sports clubs, churches, and schools. The mission isn't always the well-being of homes or families, nor should it always be—it's not why these organizations exist. Who, then, is responsible for the well-being of homes and families?

The answer to this question is now clear to me. Simply, it's the people God placed in charge—the leaders of the home: moms or dads.

My long journey to home-centered ministry helped me discover that...

Each family must learn to structure, organize, and manage itself around what it believes is important. The church has a great opportunity to help people regain control of their families.

By the way, if you're looking for an easy cause to champion, this might not be the one. If you do respond to the challenge, don't count on being a hero to your friends or family. Our culture just doesn't think in a family-friendly way.

We live in a nonstop, always-open, boundary-less world. The school churns out activities and commitments seven days a week, stores are open twenty-four hours a day, and people are required to work at all hours on any day of the week. The eight-to-five, Monday-through-Friday, neat-and-orderly community life is gone. It's been replaced by supercharged chaos.

● Almost eight in ten American adults say they wish they had more time to "stop and smell the roses," and four out of ten say they too often feel that "life is a treadmill and I can't get off."[1]

● In 1970, the average American workweek was thirty-seven hours. Today, the workweek has mushroomed to fifty-two hours.[2]

● According to business consultant Dr. Dana Friedman, work today is more stressful than ever before. At many companies, adults are not only working longer hours, they're doing it at a faster pace. That cuts into time at home and makes it more difficult to shift from work time to family time.[3]

● About half (52 percent) of all workers under the age of thirty-one say they "strongly want" jobs that permit them to get home for dinner every night. And more than half (56 percent) say they don't get enough time with their families.[4]

Simply put, you'll be swimming against a powerful cultural current if you shift your time and energy away from your work and onto your family. I often have to remember that Christian living has always been countercultural. Being a Christian calls for sacrifice for the sake of the gospel.

Let me tell you a story about something I did after my sabbatical that I never would've done prior to it.

When our girls got involved in sports, especially in high school, our lives changed. Not only was the church seemingly in control of our schedule, but now the school athletic-program dictated when we could celebrate holidays such as Thanksgiving.

Sara's basketball coach used an attendance point-system to determine who would play in the games. Each practice, every game—in fact, each basketball-related event, had a point value. You had to earn a certain number of points to start or play in the game. In other

words, the starting lineup was based on how invested the kids were in the program.

To this day, I'm not sure how extensively this point system impacted our family. But the last straw was an extra practice scheduled for Thanksgiving evening. We had a tradition of visiting Grandma after church on Thanksgiving morning. Jennifer's whole family waited to celebrate Thanksgiving until 2 p.m.—the time we could arrive. With a basketball practice scheduled for 7 p.m., we'd never make the drive to Grandma's, celebrate Thanksgiving, and get back to St. Louis in time.

I called the coach and asked if Sara could be excused. He said it was her choice but the point system would stay intact. That meant Sara might not start the next game, even though she was a three-year varsity starting guard who was in her senior year and the captain of the team.

So I called the principal. He found a school rule that said no required practices could be scheduled on holidays. He called the coach and told him to cancel the practice. So the coach rescheduled the practice for 6:30 a.m. the morning after Thanksgiving.

We had Thanksgiving at Grandma's. And Sara showed up at practice the next morning. But I'm convinced this altercation tainted

Sara's entire senior year on the varsity team. Her playing time decreased, and her relationship with the coach was strained.

Narrow-minded, shortsighted coach? Don't be too hard on him. I was guilty of similar crimes. Remember the canoe trip on Father's Day? The inappropriate children's choir schedule? Both Sara's coach and I made decisions that were divisive for the families involved.

The point is, I now recognize how my church programming decisions can negatively or positively affect families' lives.

The coach's decisions were perfectly in line with the culture's prevailing opinion: Sports have a higher priority than family gatherings. And the church often follows right along.

● How often do families let a scheduled practice or sporting event cancel out meals together?

● How often do families allow church activities to alter or even consume family vacations?

● How often do families choose to let a school's weekend events push aside a family fishing trip?

The fact that I'm now willing to do something about schools and churches dictating our family's schedule is really countercultural. We've believed the myth that schools, churches, YMCAs, and clubs know what's best for our children and families.

But don't be too hard on the culture, either. What I'm talking about isn't just countercultural, it's counter-church culture. How often do we cancel programming at the church and empower the members of our families to nurture each other's faith? How often do we excuse kids from a required discipleship class because of a family commitment?

Sacrificing your daughter's playing time on the team during her senior year is worth it if your goal is to instill the value of family and the importance of faith in her life. We must model to our kids that a commitment to God is eminently more important, and more fulfilling, than a commitment to a hobby or a sporting event.

Just a reminder: I believe the family is the primary agent for faith formation. This isn't my vision; it's God's vision (I'll deal with this in Section 5). There's nothing new about this vision—it's a truth that's buried under our culture's avalanche of competing priorities. If we stepped away from our hurly-burly pace long enough to take a deep breath, we'd see how much our culture's pace has obscured our heart's desire for God.

Rest Stop

Since each family must learn to structure, organize, and manage itself around what it believes is important, and the church has a great opportunity to help people regain control of their families...

● Does your family have a written plan for accomplishing what you sense God's will is for your lives? Why or why not?

● Does your family make decisions about the time spent on activities based on what you sense will help you reach your family goals? Why or why not?

● Do you feel your family is in control of its own destiny? Why or why not?

● What are three changes your family can make in the next year?

Quiet Detour

It's time again to reconnect with God through word and prayer.

What I need: The vision to regain control of my family life so it may reflect my passion to live and grow in Christ.

"Be careful, or you will be enticed to turn away and worship other gods and bow to them. Then the Lord's anger will burn against you, and he will shut the heavens so that it will not rain and the ground will yield no produce, and you will soon perish from the good land the Lord is giving you. Fix these words of mine in your hearts and minds; tie them as symbols on your hands and bind them on your foreheads. Teach them to your children, talking about them when you sit at home and when you walk along the road, when you lie down, and when you get up. Write them on the doorframes of your houses and on your gates, so that your days and the days of your children may be many in the land that the Lord swore to give to your forefathers, as many as the days that the heavens are above the earth" (Deuteronomy 11:16-21).

Dear Father in heaven,
Thank you for the gifts of family, home, time, relationships, my church, and faith in your Son Jesus Christ. Grant me the wisdom to honor these gifts by being a good steward of them. Protect those who live in my home, that the wicked foe may have no power over them. Give me the courage to shape and nurture my home according to your will, giving time and energy to shape it into a place where your grace and love abound. May it become a place where your Word is learned and lived. Help me to structure my life and my home to reflect my passion to follow your teaching and to pass on the faith you've given me to the children of the next generation.
Amen.

Notes

[1] from a Business Wire report of the September 1997 results of a Franklin Covey Company Research survey of 600 American adults.

[2] Candice Carpenter, "Working on Borrowed Time," Fast Company (August/September 1997), 68.

[3] Hara Estroff Marano, "A New Focus on Family Values," Psychology Today (November/December 1997), 55.

[4] from a study by Michaels Opinion Research, as quoted in USA Today (August 11, 1997).

Section 3
Six Imperatives for a Family-Friendly Church

The morning before my three-month journey ended, my daughter Cori left this note for me on my breakfast plate:

"Dear Dad:

Your sabbatical was designed as a time to refresh, relax, refocus, and restructure your personal life so that you could become better equipped to spread the gospel of Christ. During these last three months, your life has changed for the better.

"You have lost a few wrinkles around your eyes, the stressful slump in your shoulders, some gray hair, the tired look that would overtake your body, and many bad work habits.

"You have gained an easy smile, a natural sense of laughter, a more relaxed look toward the world, and a stronger sense of commitment to let the Lord lead your life and allow your work, goals, and body to just follow. You have regained your old younger, more carefree self.

"You have also gained back the love and trust of your daughter!

"I know that the Lord comes first in your life and that sharing his love is crucial. I also know that I am more important than any job. I will never allow the stress of church work to take you away from me again!

"Life very often does leave us in times of limbo and uncertainty. During these times, we are on bridges. The bridge leads us from successful, prosperous times in our lives over the times of change and uncertainty. From the middle of the bridge we can not only see the great places we came from but also the many opportunities and adventures that lay ahead. As God leads us over the bridge, he already has our destination planned and prepared personally for us.

"I pray that as God continues to lead you over each bridge in your life that your path may be lined with tulips and daisies, with few stones along the way to hinder your journey. You have taught me many things about life. I know I will continue to value your kernels of truth all the way along the path and across the ultimate bridge to eternal life. I love you, Dad! Good luck as you start your next chapter in life tomorrow. I'm excited to see where this bridge leads!

"Peace in Christ,

Cori"

It's a gift to be on a vista looking back over twenty-five years of marriage and family. I realize that only by God's grace could I be standing here.

It is by God's grace that I have two daughters who know what it means to forgive and who have offered that gift to their father.

By God's grace I was born into a family that loved and lived Christ's will and ways.

By God's grace I married a woman who lived by the covenant she had made twenty-five years ago—that she would love me for better or for worse, in good times and in bad. Her faithfulness and love didn't depend upon my actions and attitudes but on her promise to love me and stand by me no matter what.

Just last week on our twenty-fifth wedding anniversary, Jennifer gave me a permanent reminder of that promise—to forgive me and be for me, though I've caused her much hurt. It's an original stained glass panel design that expresses her covenant love to me. We've named this glass panel: "We can do all things through Christ who strengthens us. For it is by grace we have been saved, through faith—and this not from ourselves. It is the gift of God, not by works, so that no one can boast."

The forgiveness expressed to me by my family was crucial to my journey toward home-centered ministry. As I said before, it's vital that we begin the work of strengthening our relationships with our own families before we live out the principles of home-centered ministry in our churches. My family's forgiveness gave me permission to move on and address my church's ministry to families. It signaled their belief that I had changed. And how could I prod church members to change if I refused to change?

If I preach that the home is the primary agent for faith formation but I don't value the home, I nullify everything I say. The first thing my friends want to know about my sabbatical's impact is, "Have you changed? You've made big speeches, but let me look at your calendar." They—all of us—want authenticity. That means our lives must be our message. And that goes for our church lives, too.

Now, standing on Cori's "bridge," I can see the mistakes I've made in the past, and I can see a new world where parents understand their role as the primary teachers of the faith and the church understands its role as a partner with parents in that crucial responsibility.

I'm convinced we need a change in the way the church does Christian education. And our own beliefs about the home's value and its impact on faith development will fuel that change.

I used my own home experience as a hands-on classroom to learn:

1. how I could make a better impact on the health of my family;

2. what God's expectations are for the home;

3. how faith grows in the home; and

4. how the church impacts the home's ability to nurture faith.

It's this last point that we'll explore in the rest of the book.

In preparation for my sabbatical I crafted a philosophical foundation for effective ministry to families:

"Parents are the primary youth ministers in the church, and the family or home is the God-ordained 'institution' for faith-building in children and youth and for the passing on of the faith from one generation to the next."

Then I developed nine broad questions to frame my search for a family-centered church structure and programming.

The questions:

1. How will the church's vision for ministry need to change?

2. How will the vision and direction for developing faith through families in the church change the way we do Christian education and youth ministry?

3. As a minister of youth and education in the church, how will my duties change?

4. What kind of continuing education will I need in order to prepare for a ministry that puts families at the center of faith development?

5. What does home-centered, church-supported ministry look like churchwide?

6. How will other staff roles need to change?

7. How will the church's faith-development structure need to change?

8. What are the natural programs in the marriage and family area that will need to be addressed?

9. How will the congregation's vision of what the church is supposed to be need to change?

To find answers to these questions, I visited family-friendly churches, organizations, and ministry professionals all over the country. At the end of my journey, I summarized all that I'd learned into six imperatives for today's church.

Chapter 8
From Program-Focused to Need-Responsive

If the church is serious about nurturing the faith of children and youth through families, it must be more concerned and responsive as needs arise among church families. On a day-to-day basis, we must spend more time being listeners and caregivers than developers of programs.

As I talked with people about their families, I heard over and over how much one organization had helped their families grow stronger. They weren't talking about their churches. They were talking about Focus on the Family. That made me wonder what was happening at Focus that made it so powerfully helpful to people.

I went to Colorado Springs to spend a day at their headquarters. Using the nine broad questions as a framework for my visit, I came up with some specific questions to learn details about how Focus (and the other organizations I would visit) perceived what a home-centered church would look like.

I asked:

● What does a church look like that really believes the family is the place God intended for faith to be passed on from generation to generation?

● Are parents ultimately responsible for nurturing faith in their children? How is a church structured to model that belief?

● What are the rules and regulations that govern a family-friendly church's practices and programs?

● What kind of resources would it have in its library?

● What classes would it offer?

● What would worship look like?

● How would it be staffed?

● What would Sunday morning, midweek education, and small-group ministry look like?

● If the church had a school, how would it include parents?

● What is absolutely critical for such a church?

● Do we need to go back to an old paradigm for ministry, or do we need to change to meet the challenge of an entirely new paradigm?

When I showed up at Focus, Roger Charman, its Manager of Pastoral Outreach, showed me the schedule he'd laid out for my visit. Roger talked with me through the morning, through lunch, and through the end of the day. Midmorning, I took a break and went on a guided tour of their campus.

Prior to my visit, I thought Focus on the Family was basically a radio program and resources. And they are. But what they *really* do is meet needs.

On the tour, I entered a room filled with hundreds of people, each one wearing a phone headset and perched in front of a computer. I asked, "What are these people doing?" The guide answered, "Three things. Some are taking orders for materials. Some are answering questions about our programs. But the vast majority are responding to people who've called with needs or concerns."

It overwhelmed me to realize that this organization was willing to respond, that day, to the specific needs of people all over the world. Some concerns they could deal with right over the phone, some were directed to special counselors at Focus, others were referred to counselors in their areas, and a smaller number of people with more serious issues were directed to a special group of Focus staffers for even more personal attention.

I asked myself two questions:

● Why are so many Christians calling Focus on the Family for help with their families when most of them are connected to churches in their own communities?

● What is Focus doing that the church is not, and, whatever it is, should the church be doing it too?

Just from my observations on that one day, I discovered that Focus on the Family has a deep and sincere passion for Jesus and an equally deep and sincere desire to nurture and protect children. They see families as the key to passing on the faith to children. And they see the church as a real partner in that mission.

Here's the point:

Families are crying out for help, and the church is not meeting the challenge. Otherwise, most of what Focus on the Family does would not be needed.

Focus appeared on the scene, and it has experienced explosive growth since then, because it recognized a paradigm shift in the culture. Its founder and president, Dr. James Dobson, saw the deep need among our nation's children for safety, health, and guidance. As a child psychiatrist, he put his finger on the problem: Our families are in trouble, and therefore our children suffer. It deeply bothered him that children were suffering, so he did something about it—he focused on the family. And that's what the church has missed.

Many churches are still structured and programmed the way they were when the culture generally valued children and families. Twenty-five years ago when I started in youth ministry, the church and the home were partners—and many families still understood they had a responsibility to nurture faith in their children. We didn't have as many parents dropping kids off at church and going out to breakfast. Most children were expected to be with their parents in the worship service. Obviously, that's changed.

How must the church transform to meet the need? A few "souvenir ideas" from my sabbatical journey:

1. Instead of developing a course on family counseling, develop a family counseling hot line. It could be as extensive as a group of volunteers who answer forwarded calls or as simple as a dedicated phone line with a twenty-four hour answering service contacting an "on-call" staffer or volunteer.

2. Instead of funneling parents only to paid professionals, connect people to "expert" resources in your congregation. For example, link up a parent who's facing a teenager's drug-abuse problem with a parent who's successfully dealt with the same problem. Or you can create an audiotape library called Parent-to-Parent. Ask parents who've faced difficult situations such as suicide, teenage pregnancy, anorexia and bulimia, or even bed-wetting to record on tape how they dealt with their situations. Then, when needy people call the church, you can direct them to a "library" of helpful stories on tape.

3. Instead of hiring another ministry professional, consider hiring a professional caregiver. For example, partner with a local hospital to provide a "parish nurse" in your church. Already, there are more than one thousand parish nurses in forty-eight states of the United States—they offer health-care education and information to local churches. (Call 1-800-556-5368 for more information on the parish nurse program.)

The goal is to respond as quickly as possible to needs in the church every day. To do that, the church and its staff must adopt an attitude (and policies that reflect it) that puts people's needs first. That means programs won't be perfect, people sometimes won't get their Bible studies done on time, and staffers might not be around to answer administrative questions because they're out meeting needs. The alternative is to provide staffers who develop quality programs and staffers who are dedicated to meeting people's needs on an on-call basis.

Rest Stop

Remember…if the church is serious about nurturing the faith of children and youth through families, it must be more concerned and responsive as needs arise among church families. On a day-to-day basis, we must spend more time being listeners and caregivers than developers of programs.

Is your congregation serious about meeting the day-to-day needs of families? List three ways it's doing it or three ways you wish it would:

_____

_____

_____

My Action Prayer
Read through this prayer first, go back and fill in the blanks, and
then pray the prayer from your heart.

Dear Lord,

I see so many hurting people in my church. I see people who are

_____, _____,

_____, and_____. Give me the

courage today to _____.

In Jesus' name,

Amen.

Chapter 9
Staffing Properly

If the church is really serious about empowering families to nurture the faith, it must be serious about staffing properly.

Before I traveled south to visit Focus on the Family, I first spent a day in Denver at Cherry Creek Presbyterian Church. Of all the innovative ideas they shared with me, the one thing that sticks out is the way they staffed their church—I'd never seen so many paid staff positions in a church that size. (Cherry Creek is smaller than my church.)

The Bread House, Cherry Creek's youth ministry building, is located in a strip mall close to a high school and houses offices for all its paid youth ministry staffers, including:

● a youth pastor/team leader (responsible for senior high ministry but transitioning into the church's family ministry pastor) with paid youth ministry assistants;

● a junior high pastor with paid assistants;

● a young adult/college pastor with paid assistants; and

● a ministry assistant—a full-time, paid administrative assistant.

Extravagant staffing? Maybe not to some. But though my congregation and church budget are larger than Cherry Creek's, at that time my church had two paid staffers responsible for all the roles I've just listed plus children's ministry. I was amazed—I couldn't understand how a smaller church could have four times the youth ministry staff and do it with less money.

Three thoughts surfaced:

1. It is apparent that this congregation really cares about children, youth, and families because they load their staff in those areas.

2. It must be a lot of fun to have so much staff support that you really develop an effective ministry to children and youth without burning yourself out.

3. Does the number of staffers who are focused on youth and children's ministry lessen the number of hours each person works—does it create more time at home for them? (The answer is yes.) Two truths became clear to me:

● **Churches want and expect effective ministries to children, youth, and families, but they're reluctant to staff adequately because they don't understand the need. Nor do they understand that, without adequate staff, they cannot complete their mission.**

● **Inadequate staffing leads to burnout or, at the very least, unhappy staffers.**

I've presented my sabbatical discoveries about home-centered ministry to church professionals across the country. During a presentation in Michigan, with an audience full of pastors and their wives, I got to the staffing portion of my talk and noticed something. The wives had tears in their eyes, and the pastors were fidgeting. I knew I'd struck a chord in their lives. The observation was right on; these people and their families were hurting the same way my family had been hurting. Finally, somebody had named what was causing the hurt.

McDonald's would never launch a new store without hiring an adequate and trained staff. And we all know why. They recognize they could not successfully run two stores with one staff. That one staff would burn out. But that's exactly what we do in the church.

And it's just as much the staff's fault as it is the church's. Church staffers often perpetuate this dysfunctional system because they love to be martyrs or they think they're saviors. The reality is, Jesus already fulfilled the Savior job description, and no organization is worth dying for. I would die for Jesus, but Jesus doesn't expect me to die for the Christian education program at my church.

Now I know why Roger Charman gave me the book *Pastors at Risk* when I was leaving his office. Focus on the Family was already working to encourage and support overworked, frazzled pastors. They're trying to help the church's walking wounded. But it would be better, obviously, if the church knew how to prevent the wounding in the first place.

Often, the cost of hiring new people scares churches away from adequately staffing their ministries. I believe lack of money should never be a roadblock for what a church does. We let fear of not having money to meet needed expenses drive what we do. Instead of saying, "We don't have the money to do this," we should be asking, "How are we going to get the money to do this?" That's what Cherry Creek Presbyterian did.

And that's what your church can do, too. A few "souvenir ideas" from my sabbatical journey:

1. There's more than one way to increase paid staff in your church:

● **Hire part-timers.** Look for people who are already volunteering for your program and know how it works. Don't hire them to do what they're already doing; hire them to do part of what you're doing, such as recruiting and training other volunteers. The church won't have to pay moving costs or benefits—just a simple stipend.

We've used this idea to increase paid staff for our children's, junior high, and senior high youth programs. For example, in our senior high ministry, we have an extensive servant-event program that used to consume at least 30 percent of my time. This year, we hired a part-time person to manage that program at a cost of $240 a month. Now I have 30 percent more time to invest in family ministry, including within my own home.

• **Partner with colleges, universities, seminaries, or Bible colleges to funnel interns into your church.** Most schools are eager to place students in internships. In our case, I had to go to our local college for a training seminar on how to work with interns. In my supervisory role, I had a prescribed set of meetings to attend and evaluation forms to fill out. A group of us at the church also worked to find our interns housing. A warning: An internship requires you to be a supervisor—and that means administrative work. It will cost you some time. But weigh that against the benefits and all the time you will save.

• **Apply for a grant.** Our church sponsors an Alaska outreach that requires experienced adult leadership. I found out about a grant program that offered money to attract college students into servant ministry. I applied for $3,600 to cover the cost of four college students to accompany me to Alaska. I got the money. But more than that, I got four well-trained, capable people to share the load. Who's got grant money to give? Well, your denomination, fraternal organizations such as the Kiwanis Club, government social service agencies, or even corporations such as Wal-Mart (it has a fund for community service grants) might have grant money available.

• **Add the costs for paid staff into registration fees for special projects.** Last year we sponsored a major servant-event that involved over two hundred kids and adults from all parts of America. I needed a project coordinator but had no funds to pay that person. Guess who would have had to do the job if I couldn't find someone to do it? So we added $10 to each registration fee to build a pool of money to pay a project coordinator for a two-week commitment—we paid him $2,000. I just added a vital staff member and kept a few more hairs from turning gray.

• **Recruit full-time volunteer staffers.** This sounds like a wild idea, but there are people who want to make an impact with their lives but don't need a salary. How's that? Well, I know a certified special education teacher who gave up her salary to work for free full-time at a St. Louis special education school. If it can happen in the dog-eat-dog public sector, it can happen at church. How will you know unless you ask? One "yes" is worth ten "no's."

• **Hire more highly skilled people for support positions.** For a few thousand dollars more a year, you can hire someone who has both basic secretarial skills and the administrative skills you need to run your ministry. For example, I only "needed" to hire a new secretary to do typing, filing, answering phones, and bookkeeping. Instead, I hired an administrative assistant who does all that plus some of the administrative tasks I would normally do (such as working with volunteers and even running meetings).

2. Pay people to take over some of your responsibilities by working out of their own homes. The traditional pool of volunteers—young mothers with children—is smaller than it's ever been. On average, American women spend thirty-two hours a week doing "paid work."[1] Women represent 46 percent of the total U.S. workforce.[2] Many women recognize they can help earn money for their families by working in a home-based business during the hours they'd normally give to the church. So, instead of losing them to other businesses, put them to work for the church.

For example, we hired a woman to manage our Sunday morning Bible hour for children—one of my responsibilities. She recruited staff, trained them, created the programming, and supervised the whole thing. And she did almost all of her work at home.

Remember: **Instead of saying, "We don't have the money to do this," we should be asking, "How are we going to get the money to do this?"**

You can start by identifying where you need extra help. Then invite "well-connected" people in the church to a meeting. Ask, "Who do you know who could help with this need?" Then use your well-connected group to help you develop a proposal—using the ideas in this chapter or your own—and present it to the decision makers in your church before you approach the targeted person. You'll need to show your leaders how your proposal will free you up to do what they most want you to do and give you the opportunity to live a more balanced home life.

Proper staffing is crucial for home-centered ministry, and it's a hurdle I believe God is ready to help you overcome.

Rest Stop

If the church is really serious about empowering families to nurture the faith, it must be serious about staffing properly.

● Is your congregation adequately staffed for ministry? Why or why not?

● If you could add paid staff to take over just one of your responsibilities, what would you choose? Which of the ideas in this chapter would you suggest to your pastor or congregational leaders? What's the first step you need to take?

My Action Prayer
Read through this prayer first, go back and fill in the blanks, and then pray the prayer from your heart.

Dear Lord,

I often fail to trust you to provide for all my needs. And my church has failed to trust you to provide for all its needs, including

_____, _____

_____, and _____. Give

me the courage to _____ and the faith to

trust you for the outcome.

In Jesus' name,

Amen.

P.S. Thanks for covering me with your grace and forgiveness.

Notes

1 Marc Peyser, "Time Bind? What Time Bind?" Newsweek (May 12, 1997), 69.
2 "Women's Work," American Demographics (November 1997), 37.

Chapter 10
Supporting Home-Centered Staff

The congregation must be supportive of church staff in their positive modeling of Christian family-life.

I asked Focus on the Family to recommend family-centered churches in the area. First on the list was the Village Seven Presbyterian Church in Colorado Springs. I met with Roger Singleton, the senior associate pastor at the church. We talked about church staffing, a controversy surrounding the community's reaction to the church's vision, and how he's learned to balance his church life and family life.

Overshadowing all that was Roger's description of how his church cares for its staff. He told me that church staffers had a support team of lay people that met regularly with each one—not to evaluate their work performance, but to keep them accountable for their performance at home and in their marriages.

I'd never heard of anything like this. "Well, who evaluates your staff's work performance?" I asked. He answered, "The people we hire are hard-working, self-starting, passionate people. We're not really worried about their work performance. However, we recognize that people like this struggle to maintain a balance between work and home. So what do they really need? They need accountability in the sphere of family."

I asked him how his lay-support group kept him accountable. At their regular meetings, he said, they ask him:

- How much time did you spend with your wife this week, and what did you do together?
- How much time did you spend with your children this week, and what did you do together?
- What time have you scheduled for rest and relaxation this week?
- What are your plans for personal and professional growth, and what do you need from us to make your plans happen?

I reacted two ways to what Roger was telling me:

1. Whoa! These are deeply personal questions!

2. What a stunning church! This place was already applying Christian principles of care and concern to its staff. This church was doing the very thing the church teaches but often does not practice toward its own staff.

I know I was ready to hear what Roger had to say. Somewhere deep down, I was crying for the same support he enjoyed. I was in an overprogrammed church—a pattern I had helped fuel. I didn't know how to drag myself out of old and destructive patterns.

Now Roger had given me hope and an idea to take back to my own church. When I returned, I talked with my fellow staffers about what I'd learned. My senior pastor had heard about a similar idea at a conference he had attended. So we decided to do it. Great idea, right?

Yes, but it turned into a disaster for us.

Our Personnel Board initiated the idea by giving us a step by step plan to follow. We were each told to recruit five or six people we trusted to be on our accountability team. I did that. I scheduled my first meeting, and it went OK. But I quickly discovered that this was *my* meeting, and if this was going to work I'd have to train and equip them to be a support team. It wasn't long before I was stressing over my own support meetings! Unfortunately, because we didn't think through the best way to launch this new program, it was giving me more work than support.

I bailed on the whole thing. And so did most of the other staff.

The point is, there's always a cost for the payoff. We didn't count the cost, so the payoff was puny. Because it's counterculture to be home-centered in ministry, the church must be an active supporter of that lifestyle among its staffers. Unless the church is willing to support a family-focused lifestyle change among its staff members, it simply won't happen. The tough, stubborn ones will survive for awhile—maybe a decade or two—if the church doesn't get on board. But in the end, they'll be driven away, too.

We can't rely on church members to help us stay balanced. Individually, each member will urge us to value our families by spending more time at home. That is, until one of them needs us to preside over a funeral and another one needs marriage counseling. People want us to be free to turn down others' requests but not their own. That's why the church itself must help set the boundaries.

I now believe:

● **The church congregation must know and understand what it means to be home-centered if it expects its staff to live balanced, home-centered lives.**

The old saying, "Do what I say, not what I do" won't work here. But how do we get our congregation on board? It's up to us. We must express our need, set boundaries to uphold it, and then enforce those boundaries.

What would a church that responded to this challenge look like?

1. It would expect staffers to take two days off each week—just as many in the business world do—and a vacation

every year. It would require staff members to schedule these breaks on their calendars.

2. It would create a support team for the staff. Unlike our first try, this idea must be lay-driven. That means a group of lay people must have a passion for doing this and be willing to accept the responsibility for designing and carrying out the support method. (By the way, Roger's four questions on page 69 are a pretty good starting point.)

3. It would provide a continuing-education fund and encourage staffers to use it. My church helped pay for my sabbatical out of just such a fund. For every $25 I put into the fund, the church put in $75. My portion was deducted from my salary.

4. It would invite spouses to occasionally meet with the church worker's support team. Every third or fourth support-team meeting, spouses would be invited to talk about their own struggles to maintain balance in life. The primary role of this team would be to send a loud signal that the church understands that spouses pay a hidden price for marrying into the ministry.

The team could ask questions such as: Is the church doing anything to cause you pain or sorrow? After a particularly stressful time for you and your family, what's the best gift the church could give you? What are you doing to grow, relax, and refresh? How are your vacation plans going? How are your days off with your spouse going?

5. It would develop a way to evaluate how much staff time a new idea will cost to launch and maintain and then decide if it can afford to do it. Many colleges use a weighted work-formula to keep workloads in line. They figure out the maximum teaching hours one teacher can handle and then assign work accordingly. If the school asks a teacher to be a department chair, it reduces that teacher's classload according to the weighted value of that responsibility. It's a great way to keep the teaching staff from burning out.

For example, in my situation, we've determined that it takes ten hours a week, all year long, to manage and prepare for our national youth gathering. So if we remove that responsibility from my job description and hire someone to do it for me, that should free up about eight hours a week for me. (I still have to spend time overseeing the work.)

People expect a lot more from their churches today than yesterday, and that impacts the people who work for them. Most churches used to print one gray-looking newsletter and one gray-looking bulletin. Now people expect great-looking newsletters and bulletins plus four-color graphic-laden youth newsletters, family newsletters, quarterly church newspapers, and a constant stream of fliers.

Most churches used to have a children's choir and a church choir. If they were good, that was all the church needed. Now we have praise bands; bell choirs; orchestras; youth choirs; children's choirs; adult choirs for different services; senior citizen's choirs; and an array of soloists, ensembles, and quartets.

You could do this comparison for every department in the church.

Most churches used to be known for a particular aspect of ministry—great music, solid church school, compelling preaching, and so on. Now, if you don't have it all, people are disappointed. We're a consumer society that has learned to be picky—to expect a lot.

The point is, the church landscape has changed, and no one is more affected than church staffers. They're often expected to work evenings and weekends, juggling many responsibilities, while their families live by an altogether different schedule—often just the opposite of the church worker's schedule. That means staffer families are trying to live two lives at once, and that's a recipe for stress.

If those of us who've developed long-standing, unhealthy work patterns are going to change, we'll need the help of a loving, supportive church community to figure out how.

Rest Stop

The congregation must be supportive of church staff in their positive modeling of Christian family life.

● Does your church have a deliberate plan that encourages its staff to care for and nurture their families? Why or why not?

● Do you have a personal plan in place to take care of yourself and your family? If not, what are three boundaries you could set up to protect your family-nurture time?

My Action Prayer

Read through this prayer first, go back and fill in the blanks, and then pray the prayer from your heart.

Dear Lord,

Thanks for my family and church. I know they care for me because they _____, _____, _____, _____, and _____. I know you care for me because _____, _____, _____, _____, and _____. Give me a greater capacity to care for others.

In Jesus' name,

Amen.

Chapter 11
Training Faith-Shaping Parents

The church must be ready to train and support parents and the home to be the primary nurturers of kids' faith. It needs to be less concerned about building good churches and more concerned about empowering parents to build good families.

Prior to my sabbatical, I had lunch with Dr. Merton Strommen who, in addition to authoring *Five Cries of Youth* also wrote *Five Cries of Parents* and *Five Cries of Grief.* He's a psychologist specializing in marriage and family counseling. He founded Search Institute in Minneapolis as a vehicle for taking the empirical research he was doing on teenagers in our culture and transforming that information into action plans in the community. He also founded The Augsburg Youth and Family Institute to develop resources for churches to use in training parents, youth workers, and pastors for ministry in the home. I respect his ministry vision; he deeply loves children and teenagers, and I know he believes the home is vital to shaping kids' lives. I regard him as a passionate pioneer in helping churches see the vital role parents play in shaping the faith life of children and teenagers.

I asked Dr. Strommen to have lunch with me while he was at a family ministry conference in St. Louis—just so I could meet him. I told him about my sabbatical plan. It captured his imagination, and as we talked, he grew more excited about the possibilities.

Later, I sent him a copy of my plan and asked him to recommend places and people to visit and then asked if I could meet with him in Minneapolis. He agreed, but only if I would visit these organizations in the Minneapolis area first:

● Luther Seminary to talk to professor Rollie Martinson, a pioneer in family ministry;

● Holy Nativity Church to talk to its staff that had worked hard to shape its ministry into a family-friendly model;

● St. Luke's Church to talk to youth minister Lyle Griner, who was using his peer-ministry program as a prototype for how parents could minister to their kids in the home; and

● St. Stephen's Church to talk to the Rev. Tim Strommen, Dr. Strommen's son, who had developed an innovative ministry tool that deliberately involved parents in teaching Scripture at home.

(Dr. Strommen also suggested I visit Search Institute. I'll tell you what I learned there in Chapter 13.)

So I made plane reservations and scheduled a visit with each one. Here's what I learned at each stop:

1. Luther Seminary—Dr. Rollie Martinson met me for breakfast at Luther Seminary. From the moment he opened his mouth, I knew I'd found a ministry soul mate. He bowled me over with his observations about the value of parents in kids' faith development. Here are a few snippets from my notes:

● We must help parents redefine their role in their kids' faith growth. We need to move them out of their roles as taxi drivers, cooks, and bottle washers and into their role as primary faith-nurturers.

● He suggested a new curriculum for educating children and youth—a home-centered curriculum that gives parents tools and resources to teach the faith at home. It's not a home-schooling model, it's a strategy for teaching kids at home by modeling faithful living.

● He told me the church needs to shift away from its focus on imparting knowledge to people at church to training parents to be Christian educators in their own homes.

● He said, "Presently, parents take their kids to church so the church can do the lion's share of the faith teaching. We've got it backward. The kids should take their parents to church to be equipped to nurture faith and life skills in their children and return home ready to shape their kids' faith."

2. Holy Nativity—Here, I discovered the church's approach to ministry programming was based not only on teaching the faith at church but on equipping parents to be the faith nurturers of children in the home. Rather than allowing parents simply to drop off their kids to be educated by the church, the church was intentional about training parents to partner with the church in impacting their kids' faith at home.

Holy Nativity offers parent training geared to various stages of family life. For example, they offer a series of seminars—including engagement, premarriage, first-baby baptism, and first day at school—all geared to encourage and support couples during "milestone times." At the same time, their goal is to help couples understand the power they have to develop faith in their home and to equip parents to be teachers.

The point is, Holy Nativity was working to model a home-centered philosophy through its programming. So, when church members participated in the life of the church, the church communicated a consistent message: The home is what's most important, more important than building our church organization.

3. St. Luke's Church—Through youth minister Lyle Griner, I saw a church that was willing to let today's young people get involved in the work of ministry. I saw a church that invited teenagers to use their gifts as it trained them to be all they could be.

St. Luke's youth ministry program is geared for peer-ministry training. Lyle trains young people to be "Peer Listeners"—basically, small-group leaders who know how to teach, lead discussions, and listen. Each Peer Listener is expected to recruit friends from school to join his or her peer-listening group. Every Monday night, more than seventy young people show up—fifty of whom are not church members. The goal is not to train youth group leaders; the goal is to train peer ministers who will reach out to kids in the community.

People in Lyle's congregation take this very successful peer-ministry idea a step further. They train parents to be "Peer Listeners" with their own kids—small-group leaders within their own families. The end result: St. Luke's is taking the first step toward placing a trained "youth minister" in every home.

Now, if you're a youth minister, this is starting to sound like I'm out to undermine your job security. Let me ease your fears—families will always need trained, dedicated youth leaders working to help their kids grow in their faith.*

I would suggest that you avoid seeing parents as threats to your ministry; rather, see them as your well-trained assistants who have great power to influence young people. As you release them into ministry at home, you will double—even triple—your impact on kids.

As a veteran youth minister, I welcome parents' help and am often surprised by how much they value my help in understanding how to best reach their teenagers.

4. St. Stephen's Church—The Rev. Tim Strommen has developed a way to encourage third- through fifth-graders to read their Bibles at home with their parents. It's called the Good News Bearers program.

Tim and his staff give kids each an age-appropriate reading list of Bible stories and then the kids choose from age-appropriate Bible storybooks to read those stories. If kids choose their own storybooks, Tim knows they'll feel comfortable about reading them. At home, they read the stories with Mom and Dad's help. When they're finished, kids are eligible to participate in a *team-based* Bible knowledge game. The whole church gets excited about this game—and the kids love it.

---

*By the way, don't believe the myth that your job is to work yourself out of a job. The truth is that the more volunteers and parents you recruit and train, the more support you'll need to give them. You'll use your hands-on skills less and your managerial skills more. And that takes time.

Tim told me that kids will learn about Jesus at home if we change the accepted ministry model from a limited parental role in faith development to a primary parental role. In the old model, the church is the primary faith teacher and parents' role is limited to dropping their kids off at the curb. In the new model, the home is the primary faith teacher and the church's role is to support parents by providing them training and resources.

At St. Stephen's, the church plans an after-school midweek program for kids to act out the Bible stories they're reading—high school sophomores are the children's drama leaders. Tim writes the dramas, teenagers act as "directors," and the kids rehearse and then perform their dramas for one another. (So they study the Bible at home and come to church for their "homework." Now that's a switch!)

As I listened to and experienced these ministry innovators, I realized...

Parents are the key faith developers for their children—they can have either a positive or a negative impact on their kids' faith growth. But either way, they'll have the biggest impact. You can have strong faith-shaping programs for kids at church, but if you're not partnering with homes, you risk producing kids who have weak faith.

Some churches have made the shift toward supporting homes in their role as faith developers. But they're up against a culture that has stepped in to take over responsibilities parents have deliberately—or by default—given away. For example...

● **Why do so many schools now provide breakfast for kids?** In an ironic twist, some elementary schools now invite retired senior citizens to join the children for breakfast at school. Why? The kids seem "as hungry for the attention of caring adults as they are for the food," says Jennifer Cox-Johnson, a special education paraprofessional at Sibley Elementary School in Northfield, Minnesota.[1]

● **Why do so many teachers complain that they spend so much time as kids' surrogate parents that they don't have adequate time to teach?** Recently, the American Federation of Teachers targeted one cause of teachers' struggles at school: "Discipline problems both cause and are caused by a growing gap between school and home."[2] And that gap is forcing teachers into responsibilities that once were parents' domain. For example, check out the article titles in a recent issue of Educational Leadership magazine: "Confronting Dating Violence," "Peer Helpers: Encouraging Kids to

Confide," "Linking Schools With Youth and Family Centers," "Reaching Out to Grieving Students," and "Becoming Heroes: Teachers Can Help Abused Children." More and more, teachers are feeling the pressure to deal with kids' big life-concerns—and, "Oh, by the way, if you have any time and emotional energy left over, go ahead and teach a little."[3]

● **Who's teaching our kids how to play baseball—parents or Little League coaches?**

If you're thirty-five years or older, you probably learned how to play sports at a neighborhood sandlot or in someone's backyard. Parents—yours or a neighborhood friend's—probably helped teach you the skills you needed to play. Now, as communities have lost their neighborhood connections, parents have turned to organized programs as surrogate trainers.

● **Who's the more influential teacher in the home—parents or TV?** American teenagers watch an average of three hours of television per day—including almost fifteen thousand sexual jokes, innuendoes, and other references every year. Fewer than 170 of these references deal with "responsible sexual behavior," according to University of New Mexico researcher Victor C. Strasburger.[4]

● **Why, after we've worked so hard to offer high-quality programs in our churches, do more than half of the adults in a recent study of my denomination fail to have an "integrated faith"?**[5]

For some reason, many parents have—intentionally or not— abdicated their role as their children's teachers and shapers. They expect the church to teach their children the faith; Little Leagues, camps, and YMCAs to teach them how to play sports; schools to put breakfast, lunch, and sometimes dinner on the table while teaching academic and life skills; TV to be the family entertainer as it teaches cultural norms and moral values; and so on.

Few parents deliberately choose to give up their parental responsibilities—that's just the way the culture has changed. They've been reduced to a minor role in their kids' development—the captain of the ship that simply ferries kids from one learning environment to another. Are the parents in your church any different? How many of them have learned from the church that their role in the spiritual development of their children is ferryboat captain?

Parents have so much to give their children—basketball skills, cooking skills, money skills, and faith skills. What a head start they could provide for their children if they were better trained for their roles as teachers. They'll surely need help. In a Yankelovich Partners study of American adults...

● forty-two percent say their parents never taught them to balance a checkbook;

- twenty-five percent say their parents never taught them to save and invest; and
- twenty-three percent say their parents never taught them to create a budget.[6]

(By the way, there are organizations besides the church that are ready to help train parents to teach their kids life skills. The American Automobile Association is now offering a driver-training kit to parents called "Teaching Your Teens to Drive: A Partnership for Survival." The $26.95 kit includes an illustrated handbook, a detailed parent guide, and a video.)

I believe church staffers can help train faith-shaping parents if they will…

- **Transform traditional youth and children's ministry activities into experiential parent-training events on communication.** For example, gather parents for a communication-training session that covers active listening, feedback tips, receiving and transponding, and so on. Then have parents try out these skills on a rafting trip with their young people. You could transform servant activities by asking parents to teach their kids life skills such as painting, carpentry, electrical wiring, plumbing, and lawn care. I'm confident you can transform almost any youth activity into an opportunity for parents to nurture faith in their kids.

- **Encourage families to go grocery shopping together— call it a Food Scavenger Hunt.** Parents can teach their kids how to budget, what foods to buy, how to shop wisely, and how to be good stewards of family finances. They'll also have a blast doing it!

- **Equip families to transform family vacations into journeys of faith.** Show them how to turn a typical sightseeing trip into an opportunity to discover truths about the people and places they experience.

For example, on the way to Orlando, stop in Montgomery, Alabama to visit the Civil Rights Monument and the Dexter Avenue Baptist Church where Martin Luther King, Jr. pastored. Ask a senior citizen about how the civil rights movement started on local buses— you'll get an earful if you're ready to listen. That night, rent the movie *Mississippi Burning* to see Hollywood's version of civil rights history. Then travel to Selma, following the path of the historic civil rights march. In Selma, drive over the bridge where Bloody Sunday occurred. Find a local shop owner who participated in the march and ask what it was like. Go out to dinner—not at a McDonald's or a Denny's, but at a locally owned restaurant—and talk about what you experienced and learned. Then talk about God's view of prejudice and what he was doing during the civil rights movement. You'll still get to Orlando, but I'm convinced the kids will remember Montgomery.

Other journey ideas:

—Visit an old graveyard. Look at the gravestones to discover who is buried there and how they died. Have family members find favorite Bible passages on gravestones and do rubbings. Have them gather together to read the passages and discuss how they relate to life and death. Then read the Easter account in Scripture, and ask family members to each share their own feelings about death.

—Go on a scavenger hunt in a museum. For example, challenge kids to find five famous people and be ready to report on who they are and what they did. Or ask them to find the oldest artifact in the museum and discover its purpose. Or have kids find museum employees and ask them to tell about their favorite artifact and then take kids to see it.

—Turn meal times into events. Challenge family members to find restaurants that serve food no one in the family has ever tried.

● **Encourage whole families to do mission trips together.** For example, you could plan a summer servant event to reach out to native Alaskans with a vacation Bible school program. Train kids and parents to work in a mission environment, and help them to use the gifts God's given them as teachers, recreation leaders, craft instructors, and counselors. Prepare them for the challenges of communal living, and teach them about Alaskan culture, geography, and customs. You'll plunge families into situations that demand conflict resolution, forgiveness, and teamwork. And you'll help them create a memory they'll never forget. It'll take them out of a "Sunday Christian" mentality and bring a whole new meaning to their day-to-day pursuit of Christian living. (We've learned it's best to mix families and groups of teenagers together on the event—it takes some pressure off families whose relationships often get strained on the trip.)

If we want homes to be the center of faith formation, it's critical we train parents for their role. Training is such a formal-sounding word, but it can be as simple as giving parents opportunities to practice giving to their kids.

Rest Stop

The church must be ready to train and support parents and the home to be the primary nurturers of kids' faith. It needs to be less concerned about building good churches and more concerned about empowering parents to build good families.

Estimate the percentage of kids in your church whose primary faith teachers are their parents: ____ percent.

Now, let's say that next week you announce to your church members that you're handing over the responsibility to teach the faith to their children to them. Those parents will say you're crazy because (list what they'd say):

1.
2.
3.
4.
5.

Which of these reasons do you agree with? Why? Which do you disagree with? Why?

Action Prayer

Read through this prayer first, go back and fill in the blanks, and then pray the prayer from your heart.

Dear Lord,

When I think about the impact my parents had on my faith development, I feel _____. Give me the courage to emulate the good things my parents modeled and the courage to rise above their mistakes. Make me an instrument for encouraging parents to take back their role as teachers of the faith. To do that, I need _____, _____

_____, and _____.

In Jesus' name,
Amen.

Notes

[1] "Caring Adults Make Breakfasts Nourishing," Assets Magazine (Autumn 1996), 6.

[2] Robert L. McGinnis, Violence in the Schoolhouse: A Ten-Year Update (Washington, DC: Family Research Council: May 1994),8.

[3] Educational Leadership (October 1997).

[4] Victor C. Strasburger, "Tuning in to Teenagers," Newsweek (September 1997).

[5] Peter L. Benson, Ph.D.; Eugene C. Roehlkepartain; and I. Shelby Andress, Congregations at Crossroads: A National Study of Adults and Youth in the Lutheran Church—Missouri Synod (Minneapolis, MN: Search Institute, 1995), 5.

[6] from a study by Yankelovich Partners, as quoted in USA Today (October 28, 1997).

Chapter 12
A Homey Church Environment

The church needs to be less like a corporation and more like a family in its feel and its structure.

Four years ago, if you had walked into our church, you would have seen a front desk, office machines, three work-stations for administrative assistants, and white walls...businesslike. It was not a homey feel. That's because conventional wisdom in the church says, "The church isn't a business, but it ought to act like one." Even though the church should be Christlike in its activities and kind to its people, it'd better run itself like a business—especially in its financial affairs and its administration. Nothing wrong with that...unless our business identity overtakes our Christian identity. And in many churches, including mine, the "feel" is more like a well-run corporation than a welcoming, nurturing family.

Why?

The business culture that dominates our environment subtly forces its prerogatives, its priorities, its goals, its filters, and its accepted practices into the culture of the church. It's easy to see why—many of the respected leaders in our culture are businesspersons, and many of the people we recruit to help lead our churches come out of a business setting. Think about it. Who are the best candidates to lead the church—the deacons, elders, board members, and lay leaders in your congregation? I'm guessing many of them are successful businesspersons—whether they're the most respected farmers or the most respected investment bankers. That makes sense. But most models for successful business organizations are focused on building better organizations, not on building better people.

I'm not saying that's evil, but as leaders of Christ's mission on earth, it's simply wrong for us to build stronger organizations at the expense of building stronger families. We often ask homes to sacrifice themselves to keep the church organization healthy and functional. Rather, we should ask the church to sacrifice its business priorities to keep the home healthy and functional. When was the last time you went to a congregational meeting to answer the question, "How do we help struggling homes?" rather than "How do we make our church better?" We call for emergency meetings to strategize about financial shortfalls but not to strategize about helping a church member in crisis.

It's a question of where to invest our limited time and energy. Are we really about the business of building bigger, better church organizations, or are we focused on building the church through the homes where our people live?

Jesus didn't come to build better synagogues; he came to build better people. He invited himself into homes, into lives. And he reserved almost all of his criticisms for the organizational structures and priorities of "the church." It's easy for us to see his point. But are we far from the structures he lambasted?

Jesus didn't come to be served; he came to pour himself out as a servant to others. He's the model for the church. We must ask ourselves if our church structures are set up to fundamentally serve the organization or if our goal is to spend ourselves serving the very people Christ came to save. If our homes are falling apart and we're functionally ignoring that because we're busy building strong churches, we've missed the point. If we build strong homes, the church organization will be strong. But if we build strong churches at the expense of strong families, the church organization will never be strong.

Sometimes, the church weakens its family foundation by subtly valuing its organizational priorities over family rhythms and priorities:

● **Churches that schedule 7 p.m. to 11 p.m. business meetings on work nights.** So maybe Dad attends the meeting while Mom stays home with the kids. The next night, Mom goes to the women's Bible study at church while Dad stays home with the kids. The next night, the kids go to youth group while Dad goes to choir practice—Mom stays home alone. The church is a separating influence on the family.

● **Churches that try to breathe new life into a stagnating congregation by starting a building project.** The thinking goes, "People will be more excited about coming to church if we're building something new and exciting." But do families need a new building as much as they need help building their relationships?

● **Churches that easily communicate financial or business dilemmas to the congregation but have a harder time communicating about spiritual crises.** For example, we're typically not shy about bringing up budget shortfalls to the congregation, but how often do we address the problem of single churchgoers living together before marriage?

If the church adopts a businesslike attitude as its primary stance toward its people, it creates a more sterile, corporate feel. I think it's more important that we build strong homes, and the church must model what it is to be a strong home. We spend so much time and energy building strong churches based on solid business principles.

Could we find a way to do the business of the church in less time, thereby investing more time and energy building the infrastructure of families?

Functionally, is the church more concerned about making itself a lighthouse in the community than working to build up homes so *they* can be lighthouses in the community? I know that's a hard question. I had to face it on my sabbatical.

The moment I walked into Holy Nativity Lutheran Church in Minneapolis, I could tell I was in a family-friendly church. How?

I could see the lobby furniture was designed for people of all ages, including kids. It had living room furniture—couches, soft chairs, and a rocking chair—not office furniture. The furniture said, "It's OK to sit on me." The pictures on the walls were fun, family-like photos. They weren't necessarily stylish, but they said, "You're home now."

The worship area was more relaxed and "family cozy" than I expected. The altar area was down among a circle of pews and decorated like a family's dining room table—soft fabrics and casually arranged flowers. It didn't seem "churchy." The pews themselves were far apart so people could easily walk between them, so babies could crawl around, and so the pastor could walk among the people during the service.

Outside the worship area was an artificial tree that had bags hanging on its limbs. Inside the bags were soft, quiet activity supplies for children—the supplies focused on the theme or point of the service that day. These bags made children feel welcomed into their church home.

The dress code at worship services was less formal and more "family." It felt more like you were in a well-organized home rather than a place of business. It was less shiny and more relaxed and homey.

Holy Nativity has tapped into a shift to family-friendly, home-centered values that's picking up steam throughout our culture. The evidence is everywhere:

● More and more hospitals have designed their labor- and delivery-floors to look warm and home-like.

● Dentists'- and doctors'-office staffers have replaced cold, sterile furniture with soft, overstuffed chairs and warm lighting.

● Eddie Bauer Inc., the clothing retailer, has opened a chain of companion "home" stores that make you feel like you're walking into a well-decorated, upscale country home.

● Mattress companies once featured nightgown-clad models in their ads. Now many companies have replaced photos of models with photos of moms and dads lounging around with their kids in bed.

• The CBS television network has adopted a new slogan—"Welcome Home."

• More and more communities are planning "First Night" celebrations for New Year's Eve that feature activities for families such as ethnic dance troupes, magic shows, and fireworks. No alcoholic beverages are allowed. The idea started in Boston in 1976 as the culmination of the city's bicentennial celebration. It's now a fixture in 187 North American cities.

• Good Housekeeping magazine features a section called Family Life that gives tips on home-related skills such as parenting and taking care of sick children and insights into kids' developmental needs.

• In one Boston Market TV advertisement, a salesman tries to intrude on the family dinner but is chased away by a ravenous lion while the mother warns, "Don't mess with dinner"—the fast-food chain's slogan.

• Best-selling author Stephen Covey, who wrote the ten-million-selling book *The 7 Habits of Highly Effective People* in 1990, has penned a family-friendly sequel of sorts called *The 7 Habits of Highly Effective Families*. In it, Covey explains how his "seven habits" can be applied to building successful families, using his own family as an example. It's telling that one of the most popular business authors of all time has now turned his attention to families.[1]

• Three years ago, "cost of living" was the top reason workers gave for refusing to relocate. Now, it's "family ties."[2]

• More than half of all large companies allow employees to work at home and job-share. "The more progressive organizations really have an empathy for the family," says Randall Buerkle, an organizational development expert.[3]

This back-to-home trend is evident everywhere in our culture but not always in our churches. Holy Nativity's approach is an urgent message to the church:

If the church wants to help families, it must be a warm, comfortable place that says, "Welcome home." And it must be less concerned about building good church organizations and more concerned about empowering families to build strong homes.

If the church of the past embraced the business-centered environment of its culture, are the churches of the present ready to embrace the new home-centered thrust of today's culture? If they are, they might try these ideas:

• Add small-sized furniture to areas normally used by adults.

• Plan reserved parking spaces near church doors for parents with babies and mountains of baby paraphernalia.

• Hook up video monitors in "cry rooms" so parents don't have to miss the service when their babies need attention.

- Display paintings, artwork, banners, and other decorations at different levels so every family member can enjoy them.
- Create a drop-off zone with staff to help families with special needs into the church building.
- Plan one night for all of the "business meetings" of the church, forcing people to choose only one board or committee on which to serve.
- Ask families or couples, rather than individuals, to serve on church committees.
- Provide rocking chairs in the sanctuary so moms and dads can stay in the service while they attend to their children.
- Plan an annual church picnic that's geared for fun and fellowship.
- Serve people who move into a new home by offering to dedicate their home.
- Provide food for families and friends attending funerals.
- Provide a meals-on-wheels service for families suffering through illness or job loss.

The future of the church depends on its ability to help build strong homes, for strong homes will be the future of a strong church. How does your church say, "Families are welcome here"?

Rest Stop

The church needs to be less like a corporation in its feel and structure and more like a family.

On a scale from one to ten—one representing "Corporate," ten representing "Homey"—where does your church fall? What evidence supports your opinion?

What's one idea you could implement in your area of responsibility that would make your church a homier environment?

Action Prayer

Read through this prayer first, go back and fill in the blanks, and then pray the prayer from your heart.

Dear Lord,

When I think of a warm, inviting home, I think of _____,

_____, and _____. I confess that my church hasn't always presented itself as a welcoming place for those in my community. And I confess that I'm sometimes more concerned about

_____than about the needs of families in

my community. Help me to build a more hospitable environment in

my church as I step out of my comfort zone to _____.

In Jesus' name,

Amen.

Notes

[1] Deirdre Donahue, "Covey Effectively Applies '7 Habits' to Families," USA Today (October 2, 1997), 7D.

[2] Stephanie Armour, "Refusing to Relocate," USA Today (September 30, 1997), 2A.

[3] Dottie Enrico and Stephanie Armour, "Executives Push Family Agenda," USA Today (September 29, 1997).

Chapter 13
It Takes a Village to Raise a Child

Teaching children and teenagers to have Christian values and character takes a village (the whole community).

I met with Eugene Roehlkepartain, Search Institute's director of publishing and communication, to talk about the community's impact on kids' faith development. Search Institute is a respected research organization specializing in in-depth research on children and youth.

Over the past five years, Search has widely communicated the results of a vast research project that identified forty internal and external "assets" kids need for healthy living. The more assets a particular young person has, the less he or she will exhibit at-risk behavior. Conversely, the more "deficiencies" a young person has, the more he or she will exhibit at-risk behavior.

Assets are positive resources in kids' lives—like a bank account—that they can draw out when needed. As parents, churches, youth workers, and community leaders understand these assets, they can encourage activities that help develop them in kids.

For the record, the forty assets include:

1. Family support
2. Positive family communication
3. Other adult relationships
4. Caring neighborhood
5. Caring school climate
6. Parent involvement in schooling
7. A community that values youth
8. Youth used as resources
9. Service to others
10. Safety
11. Family boundaries
12. School boundaries
13. Neighborhood boundaries
14. Adult role models

15. Positive peer influence

16. High expectations

17. Creative activities

18. Youth programs

19. Religious community

20. Time at home

21. Achievement motivation

22. School engagement

23. Homework

24. Bonding to school

25. Reading for pleasure

26. Caring

27. Equality and social justice

28. Integrity

29. Honesty

30. Responsibility

31. Restraint

32. Planning and decision-making

33. Interpersonal competence

34. Cultural competence

35. Resistance skills

36. Peaceful conflict resolution

37. Personal power

38. Self-esteem

39. Sense of purpose

40. Positive view of personal future[1]

You'll notice this list of assets goes beyond the home and the church into the school and the community. Healthy homes and healthy churches are keys to developing healthy children. But so are healthy communities. Search has developed charts, books, and programs that help organizations work together to build assets in our young people.*

*For information on resources, call Search Institute toll-free at 1-800-888-7828.

As we talked about the community's role in growing healthy young people, Gene quoted an old African proverb, popularized by Hillary Clinton: "It takes a village to raise a child." The church, said Gene, must be the catalyst for bringing parents, schools, and communities together to develop a trustworthy internal compass in young people. The more we work together, the better chance we have of raising children of character.

I know that's true, because it describes what happened to me growing up without a father. I lived in a small town in rural Missouri. It always seemed to me that the whole community was interested in my well-being. The moral values my mother taught me were upheld by grocery-store managers, neighbors, coaches, restaurant owners, school cooks, bus drivers, the school principal, my friends' parents, my mom's friends, school teachers, and on and on. I couldn't get away from all of these "interested" people!

For example, my mom didn't want me hanging out at the town pool-hall. But I'd go next door to the restaurant and play the pinball machine next to the pool-hall door so I could peek in every now and then. Once I tried to go in, but the restaurant's owner, Mr. Boeschen, told me, "Benny, I don't think your mom wants you to go in there." That was enough to send me on home.

My mom always told me sex before marriage was wrong. I believed her, because the church also taught it was wrong. The school taught it was wrong. The community believed it was wrong. It communicated loud and clear that sexual activity outside of marriage was wrong.

See what can happen when the whole community works together—deliberately or by default—to uphold a value? Sure, not everyone in my town lived what they professed or even professed what I perceived. But somehow, the community's united voice left a strong impression on me.

By now you're mumbling, "Sure, this guy is talking about a world that doesn't exist anymore."

That's the point.

Why doesn't that world exist anymore? Three reasons, I think. (1) The community and the culture are shaping the church rather than the church shaping the community and the culture; (2) Churches have become islands unto themselves—developing into the equivalent of "gated communities"—and forgotten about the impact Christ wants them to have on their surrounding world: to be like salt and to reflect his light; (3) The world has grown a lot more complicated, and the church has been unwilling to risk entering into kids' reality through open, honest discussions about their moral choices and behavior.

The point is, we all need to be more involved than we are in kids' lives—involved in such a way that they're hearing the same messages about values from many community sources.

Is there a voice inside you that's saying, "That's impossible. That world is gone, and it won't be coming back"?

How can we even begin to forge a united moral front when our political leaders; our teachers; our textbooks; our denominations; our media; and our friends, neighbors, and even family members don't agree on what's morally right? The church needs to begin empowering its people to participate in the culture and to make a difference in their communities.

That's exactly what Stanford University educator William Damon proposes in his recent book *The Youth Charter: How Communities Can Work Together to Raise Standards for All Our Children.* Damon says communities should expect more of their children by providing them with a clear, united stand on acceptable behavior. He's helping communities across the United States develop "youth charters" in consultation with adults and young people. The charters ask kids to embrace a higher standard of behavior in four areas: spirituality, sportsmanship, youth activities, and alcohol and drug abuse.[2]

Often, churches see themselves in competition with community-based activities—athletic programs, clubs, and organizations. We compete with them for space in our constituents' busy schedules, and we're upset when we lose the battle. At Holy Nativity, church leaders and church members turn conventional wisdom on its ear.

The day before I arrived, the church had a worship celebration focused on thanking people in the community who'd impacted the lives of their children. Invited guests included Little League coaches, scouting leaders, youth-club leaders, public school teachers and principals, police who work with juvenile offenders, YMCA directors, and other youth-serving adults. Each person was publicly commended and given a symbol of thanks for their work with young people.

The church was communicating this message: "Our goal is to serve children; your goal is to serve children—we're in this together. We'd like to support what you're doing. Unlike a business trying to grab customers from its competitors, we embrace our neighbors as a vital part of our community." (In the next chapter, we'll talk more about this.)

Gene Roehlkepartain told me a similar story about a community whose teenagers had a generally negative opinion about senior citizens. So a group of senior citizens got together to devise a community action-plan. They decided to go to school bus stops every morning and simply smile and greet kids as they got to the stops. The plan worked. That community experienced a real shift in kids' attitudes towards the elderly. It's a powerful example of what a little movement in the right direction can do. If a small group of senior citizens can effect such a change, just think what could happen if churches banded together with community leaders to communicate a moral message to kids.

After my visit with Gene and as I reflected on my experience at Holy Nativity, I realized...

The church needs to see its role in the village (community) as a change agent advocating Christian values and influence as it partners with families, schools, and the community.

So what will it take for churches to play a significant role in impacting the community?

● **The church will need to deliberately equip and send respected church members into community-leadership positions such as the school board, community councils, and hospital boards.**

● **Church members must get involved in organizing alternatives to abortion, pornography, alcohol and drug abuse, and tobacco addiction in their community.**

● **The church must allow community organizations such as Overeaters Anonymous, Alanon, divorce-recovery groups, the Lions Club, the Rotary Club, and others to use its facilities for free.**

● **The church must equip businesspersons to deliberately live their faith in the workplace by organizing a small-group ministry that's focused on lifestyle evangelism.**

● **The church's youth ministry should be deliberately designed to train kids to assume leadership positions at school—in athletics, school government, the drama program, music groups, and so on.**

● **The church needs to gather all adult leaders who work with kids in the community—Little League coaches, scouting leaders, drop-in center leaders, and so on—and give them the leadership skills they need to succeed while equipping them to be faith-shapers with their young people.**

● **The church should train parents to impact public school classrooms as parent helpers who assist and consistently encourage teachers.**

Again, the church must reclaim its role as a community shaper. It will mean reversing the entrenched mind-set that the church exists for itself instead of for the community.

Rest Stop

Building Christlike children and youth with Christian values and character takes a village (the whole community).

Pick one:

___My church is deliberately involved in shaping the values of my community. Explain how: _____

_____

_____

___My church is involved "by default" in shaping the values of my community. Explain how: _____

_____

_____

___My church is beginning to think about shaping the values of my community. Explain how:_____

_____

_____

___My church isn't even thinking about getting involved in shaping the values of my community. Explain why: _____

_____

_____

Action Prayer

Read through this prayer first, go back and fill in the blanks, and then pray the prayer from your heart.

Dear Lord,

When I consider things that need to change in my community, I think about _____, _____, and _____. I confess that I feel daunted by what's required to bring about change in these areas. But I'm committed to living out your intentions for my life by looking for ways to effect change in these areas. Please send people into my life who will partner with me to effect these changes. I pledge to be on the lookout for them as you send them my way.

In Jesus' name,

Amen.

Concluding Thoughts

At the end of my swing through Minneapolis, Dr. Strommen invited me to sit in his family room and talk about what I'd observed and learned. He asked me question after question about my impressions of each stop on the minitour he'd designed for me.

He responded to my insights by talking about his own family; throughout his life he'd tried to be a faith-shaper for his five sons. I heard stories of family devotions, holiday rituals, family-vacation events, and family reunions.

As I listened to Mert unveil his passion for his family, I realized he was living out his vision for home-centered ministry through his family. And all that I'd learned on the path he'd sent me reflected that vision—something he'd help shape in the very churches and organizations he recommended I visit. I'd journeyed through rich vineyards, and it dawned on me that Mert had planted the seeds that produced the grapes.

First, he sent me to churches that spurred me to think about the home as the primary force in faith formation. Then he sent me to churches that modeled family-friendly programs. Finally, he sent me to an organization that stressed the church's role in impacting the community. He created a traveling classroom for me, with clear educational intent, but left me free to catch its meaning. He could've simply described his vision for home-centered churches. Instead, he pointed the way and said, "Enjoy."

I hope my story has invited you to join me on this journey and that you've seen new vistas along the way. I hope that what you've seen and learned challenges your thinking about how we nurture faith in our young people. In fact, I hope I've laid the groundwork for a significant shift in your thinking. It's a paradigm shift:

> *From church-centered, home-supported ministry to home-centered, church-supported ministry.*

In this book's final section, I'll show you what this paradigm shift looks like in the practical programs and structures of a church that's in mid-shift...mine.

Notes

[1] Nancy Leffert, Ph.D.; Peter L. Benson, Ph.D.; and Jolene L. Roehlkepartain, *Starting out Right: Developmental Assets for Children* (Minneapolis, MN: Search Institute, 1997), 24-25.

[2] Reed Karaim, "Can a Town Agree on What's Best for Teens?" USA Weekend (November 14-16, 1997), 16.

Section 4
Shifting the Church's Paradigm

It's critical we apply the five discoveries about the home and six imperatives for the church in a practical setting. It's hard to see exactly how all of this will affect the church's day-to-day ministry unless we see it lived out. At my church, that's what we're trying to do.

For the past three years, we've applied the principles of home-centered, church-supported ministry to our congregational life. In this final section, I'll share strategies you can use to consider the ramifications of this paradigm shift for your own church and then revamp what you're doing to *make homes the center of faith formation.* Together, we can work to become more effective in developing the faith of our young people, so they can pass it on to the next generation.

In this part of the journey, we've created "Construction Zones" to help you begin building a foundation for home-centered, church-supported ministry. When you see them, stop and do a little work. Or go back to them after you finish the book. Either way, be sure to transfer what you learn into action.

Chapter 14
Surfing the Paradigm Shift

I'd like to tell you a story. Let's call it "How the Swiss Lost the Watch War."

Once upon a time, there was a Swiss watchmaker who showed up at a Swiss-watch convention in Geneva with a new idea for a watch. Now, unlike the traditional Swiss watch that had a mainspring, gears, and a stem, this watchmaker's new design ran on a battery and it used digital technology. The Swiss watchmakers said it could not be a real watch because it had no mainspring, gears, and stem.

So a company from America—Texas Instruments—and a company from Japan—Seiko—picked up on the Swiss watchmaker's idea and decided to manufacture this new timepiece. It sold like crazy. In fact, it sold so well that the Americans and the Japanese displaced the Swiss as the number-one watchmakers in the world. Today, millions of people worldwide have made this digital watch the accepted norm.[1]

Now time hasn't changed—we've always had sixty seconds in a minute, sixty minutes in an hour, and twenty-four hours in a day. And we still have the same basic need to keep track of our time. So what's changed? The rules and regulations that establish the boundaries that describe what we call a "watch"—that's what changed. The world experienced a paradigm shift in the way it keeps time.

The Swiss refused to jump on the paradigm-shift train, so the rest of the world left them at the station. Futurist Joel Barker says a paradigm is a set of rules and regulations that establish boundaries and tell us what to do to be successful within those boundaries.[2]

In the late '70s and early '80s, the American automobile industry did not pay attention to the changing rules and regulations that governed success in car manufacturing. People wanted lean, gas-stingy, convenient, long-lasting, reliable, low-maintenance vehicles. Detroit wanted to give people heavy, gas-guzzling, high-maintenance, low life-expectancy, land-based battleships—the very cars that started and perpetuated the auto industry. The Japanese provided something that played by the new rules of a shifting paradigm, and they almost drove the Detroit auto-makers into ruin.

Where do paradigm shifts come from? They don't come from manufacturers or retail stores or advertisers. They're established at the grass roots of our society, born out of the needs of people. For example, the digital watch was a concrete answer to a basic desire: We wanted an inexpensive, maintenance-free, consistently accurate watch. It was just a matter of time before someone created the something we wanted, and the buying frenzy that followed literally changed our culture. The changing priorities of people drive paradigm shifts.

Think about coffee. Ten years ago, when you went to buy coffee at an American grocery store, you were basically looking at Maxwell House and Folgers. Flavors? Forget it. Latte? Gesundheit. Coffee shop? Denny's. Now you can't walk down an American city block—or through a hospital lobby, an airport concourse, a grocery store, or a college campus—without encountering a gourmet-coffee shop selling cappuccinos, caffe lattes, and flavored roasts.

And ten years ago, the only people drinking coffee were adults. Today, an innovative youth room might feature an espresso machine, because coffee is the beverage of choice among young people. Finally, if you had decided to slap a $2.50 price tag on a cup of coffee a decade ago, you'd have been laughed out of town. Today, that's the going rate. The rules and regulations that establish the boundaries that tell us how to successfully sell coffee have changed.

When the paradigm shifts, no matter how successful you were in the old paradigm, you're back to square one. The weakest competitor in the old paradigm has just as much opportunity to be the strongest competitor in the new paradigm as the old leader does.

Now let's look at a paradigm shift that is impacting Christian education in the church.

Have you noticed the number of dads taking off time from work so they can attend the open house at the preschool? Have you noticed the number of restaurants that used to be "adults only" that now advertise a "bring your whole family" menu? Have you noticed hotels promoting getaway packages that feature activities for the whole family, not just for Mom and Dad? Did you notice how the American auto industry was rejuvenated when it started producing family-friendly minivans? Have you noticed the number of joggers who take their babies along for a run in specially designed carriages? Have you noticed the huge growth in the number of telecommuters? Or the huge growth in the number of home-schooled kids? Or the huge growth in the number of career professionals trading in their affluent lifestyles for more time at home?*

---

*Trend-watcher Faith Popcorn has given this trend a name: "Cashing Out."[3] For example, in a 1995 survey of more than 6,000 employees at DuPont, nearly half the women and almost as many men said they'd traded career advancement to remain in jobs that allowed more family time.[4] Also, in a 1997 survey of Americans by Franklin Covey Company Research, almost eight in ten (79 percent) say they "would give up a job promotion if it meant spending less time with their family."[5]

What's this all about? There's a paradigm shift happening at the grass roots of our society, and it's working its way quickly into the mainstream. It's a powerful, inexorable refocusing of our time, energy, habits, goals, priorities, and finances onto the home. It's already pressuring churches to change the way they do Christian education. You've read the description of the shift, but it's worth repeating:

From church-centered, home-supported ministry to home-centered, church-supported ministry.

Let's use Joel Arthur Barker's definition of a paradigm to examine this changing approach to Christian education.

Under the old paradigm, the rules and regulations that governed Christian education were based on a church-centered, home-supported faith-development model. That model dictated that the home do all it could to provide support and resources for the church to teach the faith. The home helped the church be the best it could be. As a result, the church said, "Come to us for learning about and growing in the faith. We want to build a strong church."

Under the new paradigm, the rules and regulations that govern Christian education are based on a home-centered, church-supported faith-development model. The new model dictates that the church do all it can to provide support and training for parents in the development of their kids' faith in their homes. The church exists to partner with homes to be the best they can be. The result: The church says, "Come to us to learn how to teach the faith in your home. We'll be a resource of ideas, training, and programs, and we'll provide you with everything you need to teach the faith at home. Strong homes make strong churches."

This paradigm shift may be a little hard to pin down at first, especially if you're a visual learner. So let me paint you a picture (p. 99):

In this diagram, the church is a bright, active, and glowing presence in the community. It's the "mission station." That's why it's so full of light and energy. The homes surrounding the church are directing their energies toward the church, helping it to continue as the lighthouse for the community.

Nothing wrong with that.

In fact, for the last two or three decades, that model worked. And it worked because homes understood they were partners with the church in teaching their young people the faith, and they were doing it. What was modeled at church was also modeled at home. The light was bright at home and bright at church.

Notice, however, that in this diagram the lights in the homes are dim. Why? Because the homes in our program-centered church

The Old Paradigm:

Church-Centered, Home-Supported Christian Education and Youth Ministry

culture are working hard to make the church a bright light but have forgotten their role as partners in teaching the faith. The homes have become little generating stations to keep the local congregation bright and functioning. These homes have bought into the paradigm upheld by the church for so long: "Let us teach and minister to your kids." In the process, we've all forgotten that homes need to be well-lit as well.

In the new paradigm (p. 101), the church still glows, but not as a lighthouse. Now it's a generating station. It's busy. It's active. But its purpose has shifted. The homes surrounding the church are bright lighthouses in their neighborhoods. That's because the generating station—the church—is filling them with God's energy and love and equipping them to nurture faith in young people through resources, training, and programs. Now, the church is still a mission station in the community, but its primary function is to supply energy to the home-lighthouses that surround it.

Homes once again see themselves as partners with the church in developing faith in their young people. And the church supports that role. The church becomes the teacher-training center, and the home becomes the teaching center.

The real question is—why do some people refuse to accept the paradigm shift when it happens? In the video training-course *Discovering the Future: The Business of Paradigms,* Joel Arthur Barker says there are five reasons people resist paradigm shifts:

1. **Anxiety**—"I'm afraid I can't make an electronic watch because all my experience is with mainspring watches."

2. **Loss of power**—"I'm the number-one watchmaker in the world; if I switch to making electronic watches, I might lose my position in the industry."

3. **Anger over having your expertise made irrelevant**—"I used to be the best watch-repairman in the city, but I don't know how to fix watches that run on electronic chips; and anyway, most people throw away their everyday watches when they stop working."

4. **Doubts about the long-term success of the new way to do things**—"These digital displays are just a fad—they won't last."

5. **Jealousy because someone is better at the new way than I am**—"That young guy down the street wasn't even born when I started my business, and now he knows more than me about the watches people really want."[6]

Now let's filter the home-centered, church-supported ministry model through Joel Arthur Barker's five fears:

The New Paradigm:

Home-Centered, Church-Supported Christian Education and Youth Ministry

1. **Anxiety**—"I'm afraid I won't be able to help parents be the primary developers of faith in their kids. I'm afraid parents, and my church leaders, would never buy into this. I would if I could, but I don't think I can; so I'd better not try."

2. **Loss of power**—"Right now, families look to me as the expert at developing faith in their young people. You're asking me to give up the powerful role I've always had."

3. **Anger**—"I really know how to reach kids. You're asking me to reach parents—to be a teacher of teachers. I don't know how to do that, and I'm not sure I want to know."

4. **Doubts**—"This whole fascination with families and homes isn't a paradigm shift; it's a fad that will quickly die out."

5. **Jealousy**—"You're telling me that parents could be better ministers than me—that no matter how good I am, I'll never match the impact of a motivated, faith-nurturing parent."

If any of these fears describe what's going on inside you right now, I just want to say, "Join the club—you're not alone. You're normal. If you weren't a little scared, the paradigm shift wouldn't be a shift at all. Fundamental change typically frightens us."

It's OK to be a little afraid, but don't let your fear stop you. All of this is really God's design, anyway. How do I know? Let's look at three or four Scripture passages.

1. "Only be careful, and watch yourselves closely so that you do not forget the things your eyes have seen or let them slip from your heart as long as you live. Teach them to your children and to their children after them. Remember the day you stood before the Lord your God at Horeb, when he said to me, 'Assemble the people before me to hear my words so that they may learn to revere me as long as they live in the land and may teach them to their children' " (Deuteronomy 4:9-10).

What's Moses saying to his "congregation"? I think he's saying, "Don't ever stop putting your children into situations that will help them learn about God." Modern translation: "Don't let soccer practice usurp your kids' attendance at church. And don't bail out of your weekly Bible study—model consistency to your kids. Be first in line to sign up your kids for spiritual-growth activities, even if they conflict with band camp."

2. "Hear, O Israel; the Lord our God, the Lord is one. Love the Lord your God with all your heart and with all your soul and with all your strength. These commandments that I give you today are to be upon your hearts. Impress them on your children. Talk about them

when you sit at home and when you walk along the road, when you lie down and when you get up. Tie them as symbols on your hands and bind them on your foreheads. Write them on the doorframes of your houses and on your gates" (Deuteronomy 6:4-9).

Here, Moses is reminding parents of their role as teachers of the faith. These laws of God are so important that we're to teach them to our children as we sit with them at home, as we walk with them in our neighborhoods, as we put them to bed, and as we wake them in the morning. In fact, these laws are so important that our homes should have them written on the door posts and at the gates as "bulletin board" reminders of God's will. The point is, they should be so familiar to kids—because families talk about them so often, as well as living by them—that they're just a natural part of families' everyday lives. That's called an integrated faith.

We know what happened to the Israelites when they allowed the prevailing culture to shape their beliefs: Parents forgot about God and his law, and so they neglected to pass on these vital truths to their children. Let me illustrate with a story...

There once was a devout man who reserved each day's last hour for Scripture study and prayer in bed. He loved the quiet and warmth of his bedroom, and so did his cat. In fact, the cat loved her snuggle time with the man so much that she interfered with his reading. He didn't want to banish his cat from the bedroom, so he leashed her to the bedpost so she could curl up at the end of his bed.

The man's daughter noticed this little ritual; so when she grew up, married, and started a home of her own, she leashed her cat to the bedpost for bedtime prayer and study. When she had children, the demands of motherhood often pushed aside her prayer time, but out of habit she continued to tie up her cat. Her son remembered his mom's end-of-the-evening ritual when he grew up and decided to carry on the family tradition. But a demanding career, a long commute, and the pace of his life overruled his desire for quiet meditation and prayer. Even so, he continued to tie up his cat for a short time every evening—living out a bizarre liturgy that was divorced from its original purpose.

The point is, it's human nature to forget important things, even if we remember the rituals that surround them. History shows that God's people can quickly forget to pass on to their children life-and-death truths. That's why God entrusted these truths to the people most likely to teach them to the children, the people who had the most at stake—parents. He didn't tell the priests or religious leaders to fulfill this responsibility. He told the parents. And just in case parents missed God's point, he repeats himself in Deuteronomy 11:18-20.

Now listen to what the Apostle Paul had to say about Timothy.

3. "Paul, an apostle of Christ Jesus by the will of God, according to the promise of life that is in Christ Jesus, to Timothy, my dear son: Grace, mercy, and peace from God the Father and Christ Jesus our Lord. I thank God, whom I serve, as my forefathers did, with a clear conscience, as night and day I constantly remember you in my prayers. Recalling your tears, I long to see you, so that I may be filled with joy. I have been reminded of your sincere faith, which first lived in your grandmother Lois and in your mother Eunice and, I am persuaded, now lives in you also. For this reason I remind you to fan into flame the gift of God, which is in you through the laying on of my hands. For God did not give us a spirit of timidity, but a spirit of power, of love and of self-discipline" (2 Timothy 1:1-7).

It's interesting that Paul could see in Timothy the same faith that was in his mother and his grandmother. Grandma did her job with her daughter Eunice—she didn't forget to teach her the faith. And Eunice, having learned the faith from her mother, passed it on to her son Timothy. That's the way it's supposed to work. The gift of faith that God so graciously gives us is nurtured in the gardens of our homes and passed on from one generation to the next.

Now you may be thinking, "If we lived in a perfect world, maybe this new paradigm shift would be relevant in my situation. But we don't live in a perfect world, and what do I do about all of the imperfect people who will block this from happening in my church? I'm talking about non-Christian parents, unsupportive and threatened pastors, and parents who are not yet mature enough in their own faith to teach others about it."

Here's the point: If we don't make it our goal to move with a paradigm shift that reflects God's original pattern for faith development, we'll soon become irrelevant. And if we don't start the journey, how can we ever get to our destination? We can't let the obvious exceptions to God's original plan for families become roadblocks. For example, just because many kids abuse drugs or alcohol, we don't give up working to build a drug-free culture. Just because divorce is rampant, we don't give up the fight to strengthen marriages. Just because the world can be a brutal place to grow up in, we don't stop having babies and raising children.

It's easy to fear what we don't understand. And until a paradigm shift forces widespread change, there's a lot that's unknown about its impact. That's why I'd like to show you how this shift could change your church's ministry vision.

Notes

[1] Joel Arthur Barker, *Discovering the Future: The Business of Paradigms* (a video training-course) (Burnsville, MN: Charthouse Learning Corporation, 1989).

[2] Joel Arthur Barker, *Future Edge* (New York, NY: William Morrow and Company, Inc., 1992), 32.

[3] Faith Popcorn and Lys Marigold, *Clicking* (New York, NY: Harper Collins Publishers, 1996).

[4] Laura Shapiro, "The Myth of Quality Time," Newsweek (May 12, 1997), 65.

[5] from a Business Wire report of the September 1997 results of a Franklin Covey Company Research survey of 600 adults.

[6] Barker, *Discovering the Future: The Business of Paradigms.*

Chapter 15
How the Church's Vision Will Change

My sabbatical was a quest for answers to hard questions about how a culturewide paradigm shift toward family-centered life will impact the way the church teaches, nurtures, equips, and values families. If you remember from Section 3—"Six Imperatives for a Family-Friendly Church"—those nine questions included:

1. Will the church's vision for ministry need to change?

2. Will the vision and direction for developing faith through families in the church change the way we do Christian education and youth ministry?

3. As a minister of youth and education in the church, how will my duties change?

4. What kind of continuing education will I need to prepare for a ministry that puts families at the center of faith development?

5. What does home-centered, church-supported ministry look like churchwide?

6. How will other staff roles need to change?

7. How will the church's faith-development structure need to change?

8. What are the natural programs in the marriage and family area that will need to be addressed?

9. How will the congregation's vision of what the church is supposed to be need to change?

In the last three years, I've learned a lot about how the paradigm shift impacts church programs and church vision. In the remaining chapters, I'll tell you how it's slowly changing the church I'm now working in and, by extension, how it could change your church.

First, let's take a wrench to the engine that drives the typical church—its ministry vision.

The church's vision *must* shift from a consumer-driven focus to a partner-driven focus. That is, the church must stop seeing itself as one more "provider of goods" for harried families: "Let's see, I need to drop off the laundry at the dry cleaners, pick up some entertainment for tonight at Blockbuster, get a quick oil-change at Grease Monkey, and then drop the kids off at church for a little faith development." The '90s church has become just another service provider in our consumer culture—and the service it provides is faith development.

The trouble is, the church can never provide this service as well as families can. Over and over, studies show parents are the number-one influencer of faith in kids' lives—bar none. Of the twenty external assets (forces outside of kids) that Search Institute has identified as crucial to teenagers' positive emotional, social, intellectual, and spiritual development, half involve parents.[1]

Walt Mueller, a longtime youth minister and president of the Center for Parent/Youth Understanding, says, "After twenty-two years in youth ministry, one truth grows more obvious to me every year: Kids blossom into mature adults who are strikingly like their parents. A youth worker's influence on a teenager's spiritual growth is important, but limited—and it's certainly less than a parent's influence. Countless studies, years of observation, and the Bible itself agree: Parents are the undefeated primary influence on teenagers—for better or for worse."[2]

It's time to reassert our partnership with homes in the vital task of nurturing spiritual growth in young people. We want families to stop saying, "I come to church to learn about Jesus and how to live the Christian faith" and start saying, "I not only come to the church to learn about Jesus and how to live the Christian faith but also to be trained as a teacher of the faith in my home so I can motivate family members to impact our community and world with God's grace."

In the late '80s, my church crafted a mission statement: *"Touching People With Jesus Christ for Healing and Service."* Today, we tie in our mission to John 20:21-23. There, Jesus says, "Peace be with you! As the Father has sent me, I am sending you" (meaning you are to open heaven for everyone you can) and "If you forgive anyone his sins, they are forgiven; if you do not forgive them, they are not forgiven" (meaning God is sending us out to heal people with his love and forgiveness). We also see in our mission statement a connection to Jesus' words in John 15:5: "I am the vine; you are the branches. If a man remains in me and I in him, he will bear much fruit; apart from me you can do nothing." When we're healed from the hurt of sin by Jesus' touch, we're sent for service into the community and the world: *Touching People With Jesus Christ for Healing and Service.*

Back in the '80s, we adopted an unabashedly church-centered set of goals to express our mission. It's the acronym TOUCH...

T eaching people God's Word,

O utreach with the gospel,

U plifting others through fellowship,

C aring for the needs of others, and

H onoring God through creative and dynamic worship.

Now, since we've been shifting our church's vision away from a church-centered paradigm and toward a home-centered model, our mission has stayed the same. But our goals for accomplishing that mission have drastically changed. We redesigned TOUCH to serve homes, not the church. We no longer believe the church is the center of faith formation; that's the home's territory. And our staff, from the senior pastor on down, buys into this shift.

At a staff retreat two years ago, we mapped out a four-part vision for ministry under the new paradigm. Here's the part that relates to faith development:

"We've come to believe that the home is the primary agency for faith formation. While there are many church 'agencies' God uses to nurture the faith, it is our conviction that the primary agency is the Christian home. Every day our lives begin and end at home, no matter how our home is configured. The primary place we experience confession and forgiveness is in the Christian home. It's in the home that positive values are shaped. It's in the Christian home where joys are shared and multiplied and sorrows are divided. It's in the Christian home where prayer provides unusual and dramatic bonding with each other and with our Lord. The church recognizes the powerful influence the home has in shaping faith and life.

"The congregation supports homes as it equips them to pass on the faith and mobilizes for ministry those living there. The homes at Concordia are grace places where the love of Christ heals and cares for those living there. They're places where the people of God worship, are nurtured in the faith, and are energized to be servants of Christ in the world.

"The congregation is a partner with homes, providing all it can to nurture and equip them at church for their ministry in the workplace, at school, in the marketplace, in neighborhoods, and in places of recreation. We're called and sent to transform communities with God's love and grace through Jesus Christ.

"Therefore the people of God gather often as a congregation for encouragement, support, and training—only to return to their homes to be energized and sent into the world as witnesses for Jesus. The church evaluates its effectiveness not only by those coming to church but by those it sends equipped to their homes, communities, and the world."

To help the church grasp our new mission, we created a visual model.

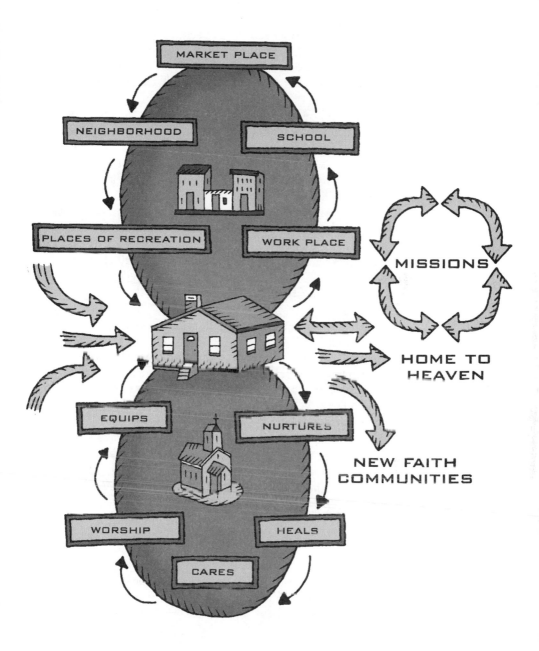

MARKET PLACE

NEIGHBORHOOD

SCHOOL

PLACES OF RECREATION

WORK PLACE

MISSIONS

HOME TO HEAVEN

EQUIPS

NURTURES

NEW FAITH COMMUNITIES

WORSHIP

HEALS

CARES

This figure-eight model places the home in the intersection between the upper and lower circles—the community and the church. Family members go out into the community and the church and then gather together again at home.

When they're in the sphere of the church, family members learn to worship together and they're equipped, nurtured, cared for, and healed. The focus is on Christ. And the church is the home's partner, helping the home to become the faith-shaper God intended it to be.

When family members leave their home to enter the community sphere—whether to jobs, schools, the grocery store, the health club, or the Little League diamond—they go as faithful representatives of Jesus. The more the church helps equip homes for their role in the community, the more homes make an impact on that community and the greater influence Christ has in the world. The church shapes the homes, and the homes impact the people who live in the community. In this model, the church is poised to impact the world through faith-shaping homes.

On the left, arrows show people entering homes. All circulate through the church and community. Some, represented by the arrows on the right, are sent out to the world beyond the community as short- or long-term missionaries who return after a time. Or they leave to join new faith communities. Or they go to their eternal home.

This change in practical vision has changed what we practically do. You'll get a taste of that change in Chapter 17—from a church-centered Christmas Eve worship service to a home-centered model and so on. The filters we use to evaluate what we're willing to do and how we're willing to do it have changed. The Construction Zone project at the end of Chapter 17 will give you a chance to practice using those filters on a program in your church. Simply put, if you accept the paradigm shift, you'll start to carry out your church's vision for ministry differently. In the next two chapters, I'll show you what that means in our church.

Notes

1 Nancy Leffert, Ph.D.; Peter L. Benson, Ph.D.; and Jolene L. Roehlkepartain, *Starting out Right: Developmental Assets for Children* (Minneapolis, MN: Search Institute, 1997), 24-25.
2 Walt Mueller, "Helping Parents Grow Spiritually," GROUP Magazine (July/August 1996), 32.

Chapter 16
How Faith Development Will Change

The vision and direction for developing faith through families in the church will change the way we do Christian education. So if we embrace the new-paradigm vision—"The home is the primary agency for faith formation"—this will mean that the church's homes will become the most important teachers of the faith. *They* will be the mission stations in the congregation. The purpose of our church's faith-development strategy will change, too. To support homes, the church will need to:

● help create and maintain a family-sensitive environment; and

● provide a variety of experiences at church to help homes to mature in faith—so family members can learn to share the love of God and celebrate their relationship with Christ in their everyday lives.

The most important discovery I've made in the last three years is understanding how important it is to carry out this new vision and purpose for faith development in *The Three Arenas:*

1. The Age-Specific Arena—This is where people of similar age gather for Sunday school, midweek programs, traditional VBS, Christian schools, camps, and retreats. It's always been an important part of the church. But the age-specific activities in Arena 1 were never intended to stand alone. They were not designed to carry the entire faith-development load in the church. Rather, they were designed to be in partnership with the home to build and strengthen the faith. If this partnership doesn't exist, we can't expect Arena 1 activities to produce an integrated faith. That's because it groups together people who are generally at the same faith level.

According to Search Institute researchers, "Positive development [in young people] requires constant exposure to interlocking systems of support, control, and structure. In the ideal, young people—via schools, families, community organizations, and religious institutions—constantly interact with caring, principled adults. These patterns of support, control, and structure function as external assets, providing young people with webs of safety and love important for stimulating and nurturing healthy development."[1]

Of course, the age-specific arena is vital to the church because it provides a way for Christians who have no family support to grow. Without family support, most young people would have no systematic way to learn the facts about Christianity. Age-appropriate classes do just that. And even Christian parents who are actively involved in teaching their kids the faith need the church's help in providing a step by step plan for learning and growing.

2. The Intergenerational Arena—Most churches now know that people need more than age-specific activities to grow. They also need intergenerational activities. Arena 2 is church-based, and one of its primary goals is to train parents for developing their kids' faith at home.

The church knows it needs to bring together Christians at all stages of faith growth for sharing, support, and challenge. Family retreats, family fellowship groups, family-fun nights, and family servant-events gather natural faith mentors into a church setting. This gives young people and adults a better chance to develop an integrated faith. Grandma shares her faith story. Five-year-old Johnnie shares his faith story. And they discover they're talking about the same God. Young people get to hear firsthand the prayers of those who are mature in the faith. Older people get an opportunity to be mentors for those who are young in the faith.

Our church is involved in a fantastic intergenerational event called the Picnic Softball League. Churches in our community got together to plan a league with just one goal in mind: to give kids and parents an opportunity to simply have fun together. Typically, in an age-level softball league, parents would've been water providers, scorekeepers, and "bus drivers." In this league, they're pitchers, base runners, and teammates. Nobody strikes out, and often moms and dads have more fun than their kids. It's so satisfying to watch parents helping their sons and daughters learn how to hit and catch a ball and run the bases. The final event in the season is a picnic. After everyone eats, we play an old-fashioned parents vs. kids softball game. At each base, moms and dads must change into different outfits before they can run to the next base. The next day we all hurt—but more from laughing than from pulled muscles.

Intergenerational activities at church can be designed to double as training events that help homes become what God means them to be—places of love and care where skills are learned through mentoring, and faith in Christ is taught and caught. When parents practice faith-nurturing skills in a church-designed activity—when they share faith stories, pray, sing Christian songs, or study the Bible with their own and others' kids—they're practicing at church what they can do at home.

3. The Home Arena—It's no good to limit ourselves to the first two arenas. The most effective arena for teaching the faith and integrating that faith into our kids' everyday lives is the home. The home is the ultimate learning center because it's where faith and life intersect each and every minute. As you know from reading the rest of this book, I believe we're not taking full advantage of the faith-growth opportunities in this arena.

To do that, the church must be proactive about training parents (that's why we need Arena 2) and providing resources for them (the focus of the church's job in Arena 3). This arena requires its leaders—moms and dads, grandmas and grandpas, and older brothers and sisters—to have a maturing faith. How many homes in your church are really ready for participation in this arena? Probably very few. We have a big job ahead of us. We must train those just starting their homes and retrain those who have well-established homes.

As the paradigm shift moves into the mainstream, most congregations will one day have all three arenas operating. On Sunday mornings, there will be traditional Sunday school for each age level, intergenerational learning activities for entire families, and take-home packets for parents who want to teach their kids at home about Jesus.

Perhaps the biggest hurdle we must overcome in order for this to happen is this: Parents are so used to the church planning their children's faith-development journeys that they don't feel they have permission or the know-how to choose what's best for their kids. Therefore, when we give them options, they feel frustrated. The solution: We need to empower and equip parents to make good choices for their family's faith development. That means we'll need to teach them about their role, encourage them to embrace it, give them training and resources to do it at home, and then pattern our church's programming and structure to support them in their role (in the next chapter, you'll find specific tools to help your church meet this challenge).

Remember, the home-centered, church supported paradigm shift dictates that the church support the home's desire to nurture the faith. This means that we do not take away from the home its responsibility for teaching the faith.

Does this mean that we do no faith development at church? Obviously not. The church must *partner* with families to develop faith in young people, *supplementing* parents' faith teaching and modeling at home. And the church must always offer faith-development programming for homes whose adults are not yet ready to teach their kids about Christ.

Since we began to shift our church programs and structures to a home-centered model, we've encountered our share of skeptics. No surprise there. Typically, their chief concern is that we're advocating doing away with the church's "normal ministry programs" for young people. They ask, "What do you do with the kids whose parents aren't Christian or with families who've just come to Christ and aren't ready for their homes to be the primary agency for faith formation? What do you do with Christian families that just won't buy into their role as faith shapers—beyond bringing their children to church?"

These people are asking the right questions, because the church is responsible for caring for those who must have a church family to help them grow in the faith.

The answer: *The church will always need to offer faith-development opportunities in all three arenas.*

Think of a three-leaf clover. Each leaf represents one of the three arenas. They're three separate styles, but they're each a part of one big mission. In fact, they're all interconnected and they need each other in order to maintain a healthy plant.

Now that we have an overall vision for what the church's faith-development ministry will look like under the new paradigm, it's time to explore how individual programs and activities will change.

Notes

1 Peter L. Benson, *The Troubled Journey,* a study funded by Lutheran Brotherhood (Minneapolis, MN: Search Institute, 1990, 7.

Chapter 17
How Faith-Development Programs Will Change

In this chapter, you'll see five real-life examples of church programs—first as they were carried out under the old church-centered paradigm and then as they now operate under the new home-centered model. You'll also see how they fit into each arena and how they overlap arenas. I invite you to try the paradigm shift on for size and see how it fits.

1. Christmas Eve Service—Under the old paradigm, this holiday activity was an age-specific event that involved only children (Arena 1). Here's what it looked like:

Before the big night, the parents dropped off their children at the church to rehearse their parts in the Christmas drama. After families arrived for the service, the children sat in groups and the parents sat away from them in the audience. Then the kids performed the drama while their parents and friends watched. You heard people commenting on how cute the children were or how well they performed their parts. Then parents and kids got back in their cars and went home.

The old paradigm's guiding principles:

1. The kids come to church to learn and practice.

2. The church writes the entire program.

3. The children sit in an exclusive group.

4. The parents' role is to sit in the audience and be proud.

5. The children's role is to lead or perform.

6. The goal is to support the church's worship- and faith-development ministry.

If we apply the new home-centered paradigm to this event (at our church, we call it "The Children's Family Christmas Eve Service"), we can broaden it from an Arena 1 activity to include the other two arenas. It looks like this:

Families are busy around tables at home, developing scripts and resources for the Christmas Eve service. The church has given each family a clearly organized worksheet (see an example of a take-home worksheet—"Celebrate the Child: A Home Christmas Banner Kit for a Family Christmas Eve Service"—in the Appendices on page 160) to help family members develop and lead one portion of the service. The church schedules one rehearsal for the program on the Saturday before Christmas Eve. The rehearsal's goals are to help families get the right feel for what they've designed and to have them participate in a walk-through of the service.

Families plan everything at home, rehearse their parts at home, and then meet with other families at church to put the pieces together. After they arrive at the service, family members sit together. They come to partner with other families to share their love for Christ through homemade dramas, presentations, and songs. There are several family choirs, and in the processional family members carry banners crafted at home. You see the joy on both parents' and kids' faces as they celebrate together. People in the audience who are not involved in the program comment on how meaningful and heartwarming it is for families to share their faith in Jesus at Christmas. When it's over, families leave for home together.

The new paradigm's guiding principles:

1. Family members create much of the service at home.

2. The church provides families with the resources they need to create their parts of the program at home. (Similar to the "Celebrate the Child: A Home Christmas Banner Kit for a Family Christmas Eve Service" worksheet, we give families each a worksheet with clear instructions for sharing what they believe about Christmas—we call it "The Family Christmas Creed." We have members of each family find an item in their home during the holiday season that depicts a Christian belief about the coming of Christ into the world. As a family, they write what this symbol means to them. Then they wrap it, bring it to church, and share with the congregation what the symbol means to them.)

3. At home, as they help prepare the program, parents and kids have many opportunities to talk about their Christian faith.

4. Most of the rehearsal time is spent at home.

5. Family members sit together during the service.

6. Families come together one time at church to coordinate the program.

7. The goal is for family members to grow closer and for faith in Jesus to be nurtured in the home.

    2. Presenting Bibles to Young People—Under the old paradigm, this activity was an age-specific event that involved only children (Arena 1). Here's what it looked like:

In a Sunday school class, away from parents, certain young people who had perfect attendance or accumulated points in a reward system were awarded Bibles. The teacher briefly explained where to find the index and the maps and asked the children to sign their names in the fronts of the Bibles. The children wrapped their arms around the Bibles and took them home to show their parents.

The old paradigm's guiding principles:

1. The Bibles are awarded away from parents in an age-exclusive environment.

2. The teacher presents the Bibles in front of children's peers.

3. The teacher briefly explains the importance of the Bible and shows the children its basic structure.

4. The children go home and show their parents the Bibles.

If we apply the new home-centered paradigm to this event (at our church, we call it "Bible Presentation Sunday"), we move it from Arena 1 into Arenas 2 and 3. It looks like this:

The church sends parents of second-graders a letter (you can find a copy of this letter in the Appendices on page 162), inviting them to present age-appropriate study Bibles, which the church will provide, to their children in an upcoming worship service. The letter gives clear instructions about how the presentation will take place and parents' role in it. As part of the children's message during the worship service, a pastor invites the parents of second-graders to join their children in the front of the church while other children gather around to watch. The pastor asks the parents to publicly declare that the Bible is important for their children to understand and study. Also, the parents promise they will help their children learn to use their new Bibles. Parents hand their children the Bibles and then are prompted to take a few moments—right where they stand—to share with their children their love for God's Word and to encourage them to read it.

The new paradigm's guiding principles:

1. The Bibles are awarded in front of the whole congregation.

2. Parents present the Bibles to their children.

3. Parents briefly explain the Bible's importance to their children and promise to help them use it.

4. Children and parents go home together, savoring the memory of a shared milestone-experience.

3. Youth Service-Project—Under the old paradigm, this youth event was age-specific for teenagers (Arena 1). Here's what it looked like:

The youth leader designed and planned a community work-project. The youth leader recruited adults to work with kids on the project and invited kids to participate. Kids and adult helpers gathered at the church. The youth leader explained the project. The group traveled to the project site and then did the work. Afterward, kids and adult helpers gathered at a pizza place to celebrate what they did. Then they went home.

The old paradigm's guiding principles:

1. The youth leader designs and plans the project.

2. The youth leader recruits adult helpers and kids for the project.

3. The youth leader explains the task.

4. The youth leader and adult helpers lead the group in completing the task.

5. The group celebrates its accomplishments.

If we apply the new home-centered paradigm to this event (at our church, we call it our "Home-Style Service Project"), it becomes an Arena 2 and Arena 3 activity. It looks like this:

The church recruits a family that has done a service project together to tell their story to interested families at a kickoff pizza party. There, parents and teenagers work together to make pizzas with ingredients provided by the church. Meanwhile, the recruited family tells its story—the goal is to give families a vision for home-centered service. After the storytelling time and while the pizzas are baking, families begin a church-provided Bible study on servanthood that they'll finish later at home. Families eat pizza together and then choose from a list of home-based service projects (for example, families may choose to do yardwork for needy church members, visit homebound people (take them a gift and lead a devotion), volunteer at a homeless shelter, or complete other traditional youth ministry service-activities). The church provides worksheets and resources to help families pull off their chosen projects. Two or three months later, families gather at the church for another pizza party. There, they tell their service-project stories with videos and photos.

The new paradigm's guiding principles:

1. A family plants the seeds for home–based service.

2. Families work through a Bible study on servanthood together at church and at home.

3. Family members work together to decide which project they'll do and when they'll complete it.

4. Family members work together to prepare for the project with the church's resources and guidance.

5. Family members complete the service project together—setting expectations, filling work roles, and working as a team.

6. Families gather back together to celebrate their accomplishments.

4. Worship Service—Under the old paradigm, this was an intergenerational event that, most often, involved all age levels (Arena 2). Here's what it looked like:

Parents and kids got up and got ready for church. They arrived at church together and then often went their separate ways to a variety of activities—from classes to choir to the worship service. If they went to the worship service, they may or may not have gone together. And if they went to the same service, they may or may not have sat together. At the end of the morning, they met at the car and went home.

The old paradigm's guiding principles:

1. The worship service is optional for both kids and parents.

2. Parents and kids aren't necessarily together at any time.

3. Age-level activities are more the rule than intergenerational activities.

If we apply the new home-centered paradigm to this event (at our church, we call it "A Family Worship Date"), it becomes an Arena 2 and Arena 3 activity. It looks like this:

The church invites parents to a training event that reinforces the importance of worshiping together as a family. Then the church encourages them to try the following idea on every third Sunday. In preparation for the third-Sunday worship service, parents send a special card inviting each family member in their home to attend with them. To stimulate involvement in the service, parents ask each family member to use a simple evaluation worksheet that uses a one-to-ten scale to rate the worship service in the following areas: music, the message, the behavior of adults and children, and user-friendliness.

At the end of the service, the family leaves to go out to eat. At the meal, the parents lead a discussion that focuses on the evaluation worksheets. The goal is to move family members toward active participation in the service and talking about faith as a family.

It establishes a pattern of connecting what happens at church to conversations at home. Parents and kids compile a list of their findings to share with church staffers.

The new paradigm's guiding principles:

1. Parents encourage everyone in the family to attend the third-Sunday worship service together.

2. On the third Sunday, parents and kids are together almost all the time.

3. Intergenerational worship is expected. Age-level activities, such as Sunday school, are optional on the third Sunday.

4. Families use a worksheet tool to promote active participation in the service.

5. Parents and kids debrief the worship experience together over a meal.

6. Parents and kids work together to process what they observed and experienced and then give valued feedback to the church staff.

5. Sunday School—Under the old paradigm, this was an age-specific program (Arena 1). Here's what it looked like:

Children, teenagers, and adults attended age-level classes. Teachers prepared and taught the lessons. Children, teenagers, and adults shared knowledge and information with their peers. The lesson for each class was taught using an age-appropriate curriculum and included a variety of activities. The teacher was the adult Christian model for the students. After class, families went separately or together to their next activity or home.

The old paradigm's guiding principles:

1. It's teacher-prepared and teacher-led.

2. It's designed for particular age groupings.

3. It's curriculum-driven.

4. It's designed to be a training session for children, youth, or adults.

If we apply the new home-centered paradigm to this event (at our church, we call it the "Family Bible Hour"), it becomes an Arena 2 training event for parents. It looks like this:

Whole families attend Bible class together. It begins with a praise time led by entire families. Adults and kids sing and do actions to the songs together. A family leads the Bible-story time in a way that's appropriate for the children in the family. Families gather separately for the "Home Huddle" time, where a family member reads from the Bible the story they just heard. Using a discussion sheet prepared by the class leader (you'll find an example of a typical discussion sheet in the Appendices on page 165), families discuss questions about the story, pray together, and talk about how they'll respond to the faith challenge for the week. A church staffer then delivers a short message to parents, usually focused on parenting tips or challenges. The group reassembles to pray, sing songs, and enjoy food and fellowship. The family then moves on to the worship service together or goes home.

The new paradigm's guiding principles:

1. It's leader-facilitated and parent-led.

2. It's designed for people of all ages.

3. It's family-driven.

4. The faith mentors are parents.

5. It's participatory.

6. It's designed to be a training session for parents.

You can come up with any one of these activities. It's just a matter of taking what you already have and transforming it from a church-centered activity to a home-centered activity. (At the end of this chapter, we've given you a Construction Zone activity that'll help you do this.)

And you don't have to limit yourself to revamping old-paradigm activities into new ones. You can come up with entirely new home-centered programs. For example, we've created:

● **Home Month (Arenas 1, 2, and 3)**—a home faith-development program for people of all ages and stages. When families sign up for the Home-Month Plan, they receive a packet of home faith-development ideas. The packet includes seven idea cards—"having fun at home," "telling faith stories," "reading Scripture," "praying," "managing the home," "serving one another," and "Scripture comprehension." The plan asks each home to do one idea from one card the first week, one idea from each of two cards the next week, one idea from each of three cards the third week, and one idea from each of four cards the last week.

Each Sunday, those who sign up for Home Month can join a thirty-minute "Home Huddle" group. The group offers families a chance to hear what others are doing, affirm one another, and pray together. (You can find the "Home Month" flyer and the faith-development packet in the Appendices on pages 166-172.)

- **The Bible Fair (Arena 3)**—a book- and media-fair in the church that features a huge variety of Christian resources to help parents to develop faith in the home (books, videos, curricula, computer programs, music, and so on), organized and displayed on age-level tables and enlivened by costumed Bible characters, storytellers, and activity centers.
- **Advent Workshop Fair (Arena 3)**—an alternative to church-based crafts and teachings that focus on Advent. Instead, we ask each age-level department in the church to prepare a table of ideas for teaching about Advent, and families browse the tables for ideas to take home and do. Tables might include plans and materials to help families design their own Advent centerpieces, directions for how families can memorize the Christmas story from Luke 2 so they can retell it at home on Christmas Eve, and plans and materials for constructing Advent calendars that feature family photos behind the four numbered calendar doors (one for each week) instead of candy or Bible verses—families talk about their memories of each photo, think about blessings connected to them, and then pray.
- **Servant Fair (Arena 3)**—tables of servant-project displays, described on take-home project sheets, that families can carry out together. These are typically the same service activities we've done for years in our youth ministry program.

Parent training is key to each of the activities I've shared. Maybe you're wondering, "OK, where's the training?" Well, each Arena 2 activity is itself a parent-training event. In each case, parents are learning and performing new skills in developing faith in their young people. This is really *active parent-training that involves experiential learning.*

These activities and events are not stand-alone programs, they're individual pieces of a bigger whole—a church-based, systematic approach to creating dynamic centers of faith development in homes. In activity after activity, parents are challenged to think differently—to take on the responsibility for building a foundation for Christian discipleship in their kids. They're doing all of this in partnership with the church, which supports, provides resources, and helps set the parameters for training.

Construction Zone

Your task is to create new ways to do ministry programs that are home-centered and church-supported. Pick one of the activities listed here:

Children's Ministry
- Baptism
- Children's worship
- Vacation Bible school
- Children's choir

Junior High Ministry
- Fellowship activity
- Retreat on human sexuality
- Service project
- Church softball team
- Hand-bell choir, band, or orchestra
- Confirmation class

Senior High Ministry
- Bible study
- Lock-in event on hunger
- Peer ministry
- Summer mission-trip or servant event
- Youth choir
- Retreat on _____
- Youth committee
- Career fair

Next, complete Worksheet 1—it will help you describe the activity through the old church-centered paradigm. Complete Worksheet 2—it will challenge you to transform the activity to look more like the new home-centered paradigm. Finally, complete Worksheet 3—it will help you record the insights you've gained as you compare the two programs. Finally, after crafting your activity, evaluate it using these questions:

1. Does the church activity support the parent as the primary agent for faith formation?

2. Does the church activity require parents to take responsibility for developing faith in their young people?

3. In the context of the church activity, when parents attempt to give back to the church all responsibility for developing faith in their young people, does the church gently refuse?

4. Is the church activity fundamentally supportive of the home, making it a worthwhile and purpose-driven activity?

5. Does the church activity in some way connect the home to the activity?

(Each of these church activities assumes that the church will help by providing resources and training for parents to teach the faith at home.)

Worksheet 1—Describing a Church-Centered Program

Church Program _____

What does this "church-centered" program look like? Write a
short description of how it expresses the church-centered paradigm.

What old-paradigm "Guiding Principles" direct this program?

1.

2.

3.

4.

5.

6.

7.

Worksheet 2—Describing a Home-Centered Program

Church Program _____
What would this same program look like if you transformed it by using the "home-centered" paradigm? Write a short description.

What new-paradigm "Guiding Principles" would direct this program?

1.

2.

3.

4.

5.

6.

7.

Worksheet 3—Gaining Insights

Church Program _____

Write the insights you've gained about the differences between the old-paradigm model for this program and the new-paradigm model you created.

List questions you have about the home-centered vs. church-centered approach to this program.

Invite someone on your church staff or a lay leader to have a cup of coffee (or a beverage of choice) with you and talk about what you've learned and what you're still struggling with.

Congratulations! You've taken a first step toward helping the home to be a powerful center for faith formation in partnership with the church.

Chapter 18
A New Church Position: Family Minister

As ministers of youth and education in the church, we can't continue to do what we've always done and expect our church to move toward the home-centered model. That's why my church created a new position with a new title and new responsibilities—Minister to the Christian Home. In this chapter, I'll detail my new duties with a particular focus on a big shift in my ministry—parent education and training. I'll also address an obvious need that's born out of shifting job requirements—continuing education.

First, let's tackle my new job description. It describes how I live out the paradigm shift in my everyday duties:

"The Minister of the Christian Home will assist parents with children and teenagers in the growth of their homes as homes of faith and grace. This will happen by planning, developing, and implementing a coordinated way for the Christian home to be the primary agency for faith formation.

"Homes are vital institutions to this faith community—they are the faith-teaching stations. Our homes provide the primary environment for our people to live out their faith. Our homes are light and salt for others to see Jesus and experience God and his love.

"The Minister of the Christian Home will:

● "Help homes be centers for the growth of the Christian faith, and help equip parents with faith-filled parenting and couple-relationship skills;

● "Open opportunities for homes to live out God's will and love in their everyday lives—enabling home networks and providing Christian resources to help homes pass on the faith from one generation to the next;

● "Motivate the people of the church to be Christian stewards of children—our most precious gift—who give of themselves in service to God and neighbor;

● "Encourage homes to display their love for God and each other as a witness to Christ's love in their neighborhood;

● "Support God's plan for marriage and the family as the primary agency for faith formation;

● "Lift up, develop, and carry out an action plan for ministry, working with the pastor, staff, and congregation—based on our vision for homes as the primary agencies for faith formation; and

● "Ensure that each home has the opportunity to know and live out God's will, creating a place where God's love abounds for all who live there and enabling—through the power of the Spirit—the faith to be passed on from one generation to the next."

These are my general responsibilities.* But we needed a way to coordinate them churchwide. Obviously, much of what I do impacts other ministry areas and other staffers—particularly the roles of children's minister, junior high minister, and senior high minister. So we created a plan to guide and set parameters for this new area of ministry in the church. The plan details areas of responsibility and pairs them with goals and activities. Here's what it looks like in a Target-Goal-Activities format:

Critical Target 1:
A home-centered, church-supported faith-development system.
Goal:
To reshape our faith-development programs, activities, and structure to be home-centered and church-supported.
Activities:
● **Reshape all of the church's faith-development programs to be home-centered through a series of planning events.** Programs to reshape include our "Sunday Morning Bible Hour," midweek programs, vacation Bible school and camp, the junior high confirmation ministry, and the senior high youth group.

● **Develop new programming that is home-centered.** Sunday mornings will need to feature strong intergenerational activities that are family-friendly. Classes should be focused on learning and supporting each other as we nurture the faith in our homes. Plan an annual family camp that models home-centered faith development. Encourage homes to offer family members' gifts, such as music, drama, and art, to the congregation in intergenerational settings. Plan servant events that are tailored for entire families.

● **Help all boards and committees think and plan for home-centered ministry.** Plan intergenerational events focused on the community in order to network, model, and grow in our understanding of the home's powerful influence on young people. Events will include the Advent Devotional Fair, our annual Recommitment to Marriage event, the Home Servant-Fair/Bible Fair, our Family Fun Festival, regional picnics, and family camp.

● **Lead a planning event for all of the church's program boards to help them reshape themselves for home-centered, church-supported ministry.**

---

*I'm often asked for copies of my new job description and those of our junior high and senior high ministers. I've included them in the Appendices on pages 154–159.

Critical Target 2:
Teaching parenting skills.
Goal:
To equip parents with faith-nurturing and parenting skills.
Activities:

● **Form and recruit members for a new "parent faith-development board" and then turn it loose to create a "family university" for the church.** Using the expertise of its members, the board should create courses that help equip parents to build strong homes.

Faith-development classes could include: "Renewing the Family Spirit," "The Spiritual Gifts of Children," "Shaping My Home Deliberately," "Faith-Shaping Skills," "Value-Centered Parenting," and "Building Assets in Youth."

Parenting classes could include: "Discipline," "Money Management," "Communication," "On Being Father," "On Being Mother," "Homework-Skills Development," "Developing Servant Hearts," "Being Good Stewards," "Age-Level Development," "Parenting an Infant," "Parenting a Toddler," "Parenting in the Early-Childhood Years," "Parenting in the Elementary Years," "Parenting the Junior Higher," "Parenting the Senior Higher," "Parenting the College Student," and "Equipping My Kids With Life Skills."

● **Create a "milestone ministry" to support and encourage homes in all of life's stages.** Ministry activities could include seminars and retreats on: pre-engagement, pre-baptism, a child's first day in school, preparing for confirmation, leaving for college, wedding preparation, the first grandchild, retirement, and parenting your parent.

● **Host annual major seminars or conferences on the family.** Topics could include premarriage and marriage enrichment.

Critical Target 3:
Enriching and strengthening marriages.
Goal:
To equip Christian couples for lifelong marriages.
Activities:

● **Provide resources and training for married couples through retreats, seminars, and ongoing classes.** Training events could include: marriage encounters, marriage-enrichment seminars, couples-dialogue retreats, and premarriage counseling.

Critical Target 4:
Mentoring the leaders of the home.
Goal:
Recruit, train, and make available to church families "mentoring homes."

Activities:

● **Develop a systematic faith-development system to support church homes in teaching their children and teenagers.**

● **Develop a congregational small-group ministry that's built around issues concerning homes.**

● **Develop support groups for homes.** Groups could be focused for single parents, divorced men and women, those grieving over a loss, men as fathers and husbands, women as mothers and wives, couples in marriage, families with a first child in high school or college, families caring for an aging parent, and retirees.

Critical Target 5:
Provide resources for home faith-development.
Goal:
Make the church a "home resource center" that offers families access to helpful faith-development tools.
Activities:

● **Plan for a large "family resource room."** This should be a place where families can purchase, rent, and exchange audiotapes, videos, and books that will help them become all they can be.

● **Publish a newsletter for homes.** Include helpful information on teaching the faith at home, life-skills information, statistics, resource announcements, helpful phone numbers, and advice.

● **Plan home-centered fairs.** Give families the chance to do "one-stop shopping" for home faith-development ideas. Fair themes could include Advent, Easter, Bible study, and prayer.

As I mentioned at the start of this chapter, parent education and training is now a big part of what I do. That only makes sense. But I'm not really a marriage- and family-professional. I'm an educator whose mission in life is to *nurture faith in Jesus Christ in children and teenagers through families in the church for a better tomorrow.* I know I need further training to prepare for this new challenge (more on this a bit later). Meanwhile, I know I must work to help couples build strong marriages and families if their homes are to be training stations for Christian education.

So we've started to focus on this goal through a program we call Milestone Ministry. Through it, we offer homes a series of growth-oriented events that are geared to promote faith development and offer support at various important life-stages. I've already mentioned some of these events in the ministry plan. Our aim is to provide home-centered training for parents in faith formation. We define a milestone event by four criteria:

1. It must have the potential for increasing stress on individuals in the home or for significantly impacting their spiritual lives.

2. It must involve a significant life-change—spiritual, physical, intellectual, emotional, or social.

3. It must be a time when the church can have, or needs to have, a significant impact in the lives of families.

4. It must be a time in an individual's life that creates a desire for information and support.

Using these guidelines, we've identified several "milestones" in our families' lives, and so far, we've designed programs to target two of them. Church members lead and serve as teachers for each program.

● **Pre-Cana**—a Saturday event for couples planning to marry. During the day, they learn about the theology of marriage, communication skills, medical issues, financial planning, and the role of the home in faith formation. They also fill out a "compatability inventory" called "Prepare and Enrich" and then enjoy dinner with married couples who talk about their joys and sorrows as married people.

● **Pre-Baptism**—also a Saturday event, designed for couples preparing for the birth of their first child. They learn about the theology of baptism, participate in a "practice run" for their child's baptism, and receive resources and training that will help them make their home the center of faith development for their child. We also offer couples time to do a "checkup" on their marriage relationships.

In the future, we'll be developing Milestone Ministry programs called:

● **Before We Start School**—an event that will help families prepare to partner with their children's teachers in shaping children's lives.

● **The Changes of Puberty**—designed to help families understand the cataclysmic changes young adolescents experience and the choices those changes force.

● **Independence Day: I'm In High School!**—for teenagers entering senior high and their parents.

● **I'm Going to Be the Parent of a College Student**—for parents of incoming freshmen.

We also hope to add Milestone Ministry programs for parents whose first child is about to marry, for sons and daughters experiencing the death of a parent, for families that have moved to a new city, for adults who change jobs or lose jobs, for families enduring a medical crisis, for parents experiencing an "empty nest," for adults who retire, and for adults who must "parent" their own parents late in life.

Our goal through all of these milestone activities is to be deliberate about helping families develop faithful people in their homes, giving them support to fulfill their responsibilities, and building spiritual leaders throughout the life span.

Key to all of this is, of course, a well-coordinated parent-education curriculum. I'm not qualified to develop it, but we've recruited experts in our church to serve on a "parent nurture board." They'll map out a series of classes that focus on the development stages of a child's life.

We're also working to reconnect the "natural mentors" in kids' lives—fathers, mothers, grandparents, and other relatives—to young people looking for answers to big questions. And we're gathering adults to serve as mentors for kids who have no natural mentors in their lives.

On a retreat for families interested in developing their own mission statements and goals, we ask an over-sixty-five senior adult to serve as a mentor for each small group of three couples. The mentors are there to offer perspective drawn from their own life experiences. The couples love it.

How can we connect mentors to needy people more often? I know many churches that match mentor couples with engaged couples participating in a premarriage counseling program. And I know churches that connect childless men to fatherless young people for father/son and father/daughter events. It's simply not that difficult to brainstorm ways to connect those who have something valuable to give to those who need something valuable.

Finally, we're just now beginning to filter men's and women's ministry priorities through a family-friendly filter. Who knows what exciting new ways we'll find to help men and women grow in their unique ability to give to their children, family, friends, neighbors, and co-workers? Already, home-centered ministries to men and women are gathering significant cultural steam—witness the explosive growth and influence of Promise Keepers and M.O.P.S.

Now, what new skills will we need to prepare for a ministry that puts families at the center of faith development?

On my sabbatical, I visited schools that offer master's degree programs in family studies and master's degree programs in marriage and family counseling. In general, the family-studies programs focus on how to prevent disasters in homes—they teach you how to be a family-life educator. On the other hand, the marriage- and family-counselor programs focus on repairing broken relationships.

I haven't yet decided which way to go. Both paths have advantages and disadvantages. I've discovered the counseling path garners more respect among family-focused professionals. I asked Merton Strommen for a little advice. He told me that if I want credibility among my peers, the counseling route is the best one to travel. The negative, however, is that you must invest many hours in clinical-counseling work to gain that degree. And most of us will be more involved in teaching than in counseling at church.

In the end, my choice will depend on what I decide to aim for. Right now, my heart says that people in the church need what a family-studies program (with a theological component) can offer more than they need what a marriage- and family-counseling program can offer. Either way, retraining is important. Think of it as an investment in your greatest asset—you.

Let me stress that we're still learning what it means to meet the challenge of the paradigm shift. Your target areas may be different than ours because your church's needs are unique. But if you understand the differences between my old and new responsibilities, you'll know how to get started revamping your own. Essentially, I moved...

● from stepping into parents' responsibilities to equipping parents to do their job;

● from fixing teenagers' broken lives to connecting homes with resources that will help them repair their own brokenness;

● from setting myself up as the only resource to making many resources available to families;

● from doing the ministry to managing ministry through the gifts of the people of God; and

● from responding to concerns, complaints, and ideas about programs to simply leading the ministry.

Home-centered ministry takes seriously the real-world needs of parents and families. It finds ways to partner with parents in creating homes that overflow with grace and love. It sees families clearly and offers love, wisdom, and support freely.

This is an empowering, encouraging, and far more efficient approach to church ministry. We've worn ourselves out trying to do what families will always do better than us.

Let's say your favorite team's quarterback goes down with a broken ankle and his backups are already out with the flu. So the coach decides he has no other choice but to play quarterback himself. Now, the coach may do a great job, considering the demanding situation he's been thrown into, but he's a great coach, not a great starting quarterback. The team's going to bog down. The sooner the injured first-stringer makes it back into the lineup, the better the team will perform.

When we embrace the paradigm shift and start supporting parents in their faith-training role, we're like the coach encouraging the quarterback to get back into the game.

Chapter 19
Churchwide Implications

Of course, when your church shifts to a home-centered model, more than your Christian education program will need to change. Let's take a quick look at the areas of worship, stewardship, evangelism, fellowship, and service. You'll get a glimpse into the impact of the paradigm shift on each area.

Before we launch into this, consider the key question leaders in each area must ask themselves: "How is what we're doing at church affecting the homes of the people we're serving?" For example: "Will the time we choose for the activity be family-friendly?" (not scheduled during prime family hours) or "Will the very nature of the activity communicate that homes are important?" (such as retreats that keep families together for most of the event).

Worship Service
Home-centered worship leaders recruit whole families as volunteer helpers whenever possible—as ushers, Communion servers, choir members, special-music performers, and Scripture readers. The worship environment—the seating arrangement, sight lines, music, message, prayers, and so on—must be planned with the whole family in mind. If any family member feels excluded from something in the worship service, it's not family-friendly.

Stewardship
When home-centered church leaders plan a stewardship drive, they're thinking of ways to educate whole families about giving. Instead of simply asking for money, we can help families learn how to become financially secure. We can offer programs that help each family member develop positive Christian financial patterns in his or her life—including God's expectations for giving. *A home-centered stewardship drive* would give families opportunities to learn ways to manage their time, talents, and assets.

Evangelism
Home-centered evangelism helps families be lighthouses in their neighborhoods by teaching them how to share their Christian faith together. *A home-centered evangelism drive* might include family-sponsored neighborhood parties that feature Christian dramas performed by the children and their neighborhood friends. Or families might get together to plan and perform a special drama or con-

cert at church with the sole purpose of inviting neighborhood families to come and watch.

Fellowship
So often our fellowship activities target age groups. That's important, but families are hungry for opportunities to be together, too! Create family fellowship events that help families have fun, learn new skills, and connect to others in the congregation along the way. How about a bike trip for families? a bowling night? a scavenger hunt? At each event, make sure to give family leaders parenting tips, resources, and ideas to use at home.

Service
Search Institute's research into external assets found that homes that serve together create more than great memories—they build great families.[1] So how can the church structure its outreach activities to help families offer their gifts to the church and community? Instead of asking families to fix up the church, how about helping families serve each other? What would it say to families in need if church families gathered for a modern "barn raising"—putting on a new roof or painting a house? What would it say to junior highers if moms and dads decided to serve their kids by helping them with their chores at home—such as cleaning their rooms?

Clearly, the deeper we move into home-centered ministry, the more the church itself will change. The paradigm shift will fuel new roles and new ministries. It has in our church. And when that happens, it's important to integrate them into a unified team.

Your present staffers will need to refocus…

● from *being* the ministry to equipping the ministry;

● from *being* the answer to connecting homes to the answer;

● from *being* the resource to providing resources;

● from *doing* the ministry to managing the ministry through the God-given gifts of the people; and

● from *responding* to concerns, complaints, and ideas about programs to leading the charge for the new vision.

For example, under the new paradigm your music minister may provide training and resources for families to sing at home. A church-based nurse may train families to provide home health-care and train first-time mothers to minister to their new babies. Your children's minister may develop resources for moms and dads to develop their kids' faith at home.

If your church is large, new staff positions may include a marriage-and family-counselor, a social worker, and a full-time administrator for your family resource center.

How will your church integrate all this newness? We had to tweak our internal structure to reflect our new vision for ministry.

Four years ago, we had an independent age-level education system—an Arena 1 program that basically isolated age groups from each other. Our children's ministry was independent from junior high ministry, and adult education was independent from senior high ministry. Now we've shifted to a structure that models our vision for home-centered ministry. The structure's centerpiece is a coordinating council that focuses on the needs of *all* homes—from those just getting started to those who've worked together for years.

The coordinating council oversees age-level task forces for children's ministry, junior high ministry, senior high ministry, adult education, and seniors ministry. Each task force meets separately but all are shaped by the council to uphold our shared vision through coordinated goals.

Using this structure, the council can coordinate activities and events that include many age levels, such as the Bible Fair described in Chapter 17. The council sets the program's parameters, and each age-level task force is responsible for providing materials and activities for its age group. For example, when the coordinating council plans a Thanksgiving homebound luncheon for senior citizens at the church, it can delegate responsibilities to both the seniors task force and the junior high task force.

In a sense, we've turned our faith-development system on its end. We used to think only in terms of age groups; now we're thinking in terms of life spans.

The second major shift we've made is administrative. Frankly, we used to try to control what went on in each age-level area—since the church was at the center of faith development, we played traffic cop for every program, activity, and event. Now we try to encourage people to run with their own ideas by equipping them and then removing roadblocks and hoops from their path. This permission-giving attitude has spurred many exciting new activities at our church. That's how our Home Month emphasis and Family Bible Hour got started.

But permission-giving works only if the congregation understands the paradigm shift and embraces the church's new role. The truth is, not everyone wears a digital watch. Not everyone pays $2.50 for a cup of coffee. And not everyone will embrace a home-centered ministry philosophy in the church—especially since we've spent decades teaching homes to rely on the church to provide for all their faith-development needs.

If we're to be successful at "remembering God"—at passing on the faith to the next generation—we'll need to help our congregations see the shift toward family-focused ministry and assume their role as teachers of the faith. We'll need to paint a living picture of the church as...

- a training station, not just a teaching station;
- a place where programs and activities declare that people of all ages and stages are welcome and important;
- a mentoring community willing to share its time and expertise for the sake of families;
- a change agent in the community, advocating a home-centered approach to issues and priorities;
- a resource for all kinds of family needs; and
- an on-call support for struggling families.

As we help our people embrace a new vision for the church's role as a home supporter in faith development, they'll begin to see their homes as...

- faith-shapers in partnership with a supportive church;
- neighborhood mission-stations that proclaim the message of God's love, grace, forgiveness, and eternal life;
- servants of Jesus, passionate about his priorities; and
- magnets for people seeking truth, kindness, and love.

As homes transform into lighthouses in the community, parents will begin to see themselves as...

- teachers of the faith, well-prepared to pass it on to their children;
- models of Christlike love—mirrors that reflect the power of Christ at work in sin-scarred people;
- proactive in growing their marriages and in learning skills to lead their families; and
- responsible caretakers who place family members before work and before pleasure.

If the people of Christ do what it takes to make this shift, we'll see succeeding generations honor God with their lives. And it all starts with us—it's what we model in our own homes, the boundaries we set as church staffers, the filters we use in ministry, and the priorities we live out when no one's watching. That's why I could never talk about changing the church until I got to work changing my own family. It's why Jesus warned, "What good will it be for a man if he gains the whole world, yet forfeits his soul?" (Matthew 16:26a).

I've already said that the shift to home-centered ministry is counterculture and counter-church-culture. Almost by default, churches that make the shift will be swimming upstream—and that's their historic role in society. If your church takes on the challenge, relish it. You'll quickly become an advocate for families through the schools, through community programs, in the workplace, and in the marketplace. What a privilege!

We'll work together to counter the corporate "burn and turn" attitude toward employees. We'll help reshape schools from hostile competitors with homes to supportive partners with homes, and we'll urge the marketplace to adopt home-friendly schedules and home-friendly environments. *Simply, the church's role in the culture is to be an advocate for homes and those that live in them.*

The mission starts with you, and there are plenty of things you can do right away. For example, you can:

● **Be proactive about teaching the faith at home.** Learn to see the things that happen in your home as jumping-off points for teaching about the gospel. In the spring, when the plants are poking through the ground, connect what you see to the Resurrection. When you hear a siren, gather the family to say a prayer for the situation. When you're watching TV, during the commercials, talk about the faith issues the characters raise.

● **Be willing to challenge schools, your community, and your church when they continue to divide your family with their schedules and programming.** You don't have to change these institutions, but you can begin advocating for a more family-friendly way to approach what they do.

● **If you aren't consistently reading your Bible and modeling it for your kids, start now.** Encourage your kids to follow your personal Bible study patterns.

● **Embrace the fact that you are the primary influence on your children.** Recognize that your "primary influence" can be negative or positive. You may not be able to change other institutions, but you can change your own home.

Conclusion

Twenty-five years ago, I walked into Shore Haven Church and settled into a little office with a "youth minister" nameplate on the door. In those early days, I remember asking myself an honest question: "What is youth ministry, anyway?" I asked the kids I served. I asked the adults in the church. It was my quest—to understand the role God had given me.

Today, I'm a minister to the Christian home, and I've replaced one quest with another. Or maybe I've discovered the two quests follow the same path. Youth ministry and family ministry have at their heart an overarching mission: to teach children and teenagers to love God with all their hearts, souls, and mind and to love their neighbors as themselves.

And I believe, in this generation, the best way to accomplish this mission is to equip and train the home's leaders to fulfill it—whether it's moms and dads, brothers and sisters, aunts and uncles, or grandmas and grandpas. As these leaders learn to teach the faith with passion and clarity, the next generation will know without a doubt that Jesus Christ is Savior of the world and that his death and resurrection purchased their forgiveness, their life eternal.

It's the right time to return to God's vision for "remembering" his great love for his people—to partner with homes to grow faith-filled, faithful people whose lives reflect Jesus.

Sure, family ministry includes parenting classes, marriage enrichment, marriage counseling, couples dialogues, home-management courses, pre-engagement seminars, family retreats, and marriage-anniversary celebrations. But we must never forget why we do these things—to foster, in a place called the home, a safe and faithful place. A place that helps young people sense God's wonder and grace and experience his tender touch, the forgiveness of sins, the mystery of prayer, the power of God's Word, and the compelling desire to worship him.

All of this we do in preparation for entering our heavenly home—where someday I will meet both my Father in heaven and my earthly father. I look forward to this great meeting because my mother, my brother, and my sisters took seriously their responsibility to encourage my relationship with Jesus.

May God bless your ministry and your home as you labor with love to pass on the faith to the next generation.

Construction Zone

So you're convinced it's time to embrace the new paradigm for home-centered ministry. How do you convince your church leaders to get on board? First you have to create a "vacuum for change," as Merton Strommen called it. Use the following outline to develop a presentation that will invite your church to begin the journey.

1. Tell how you currently do faith-development ministry in your church, and report its results.

When I did this, I used the ministry acronym TOUCH that I've referred to already. Here's what I did:

T is for Teaching the faith. "We ask our people to come to church to learn about Jesus."

O is for Outreach with the gospel message. "We ask our people to come to church to learn how to evangelize."

U is for Uplifting each other in fellowship. "We ask our people to come to church for all of the Christian fellowship they'll ever need."

C is for Caring for the needs of others. "We ask our people to come to church to participate in service projects."

H is for Honoring God in dynamic worship. "We ask our people to come to church to learn how to worship God."

I then told church members that, though our numbers looked fine, we were not having the kind of impact a church of our size should have. Also, I told them that the teenagers who were really making significant commitments to Christ were mostly from committed Christian homes.

2. Using the "What Does a Model Teenager's Faith Look Like?" worksheet (found in the Appendices, page 146), ask church members to describe a model teenager who's participated in the church's ministry.

After they fill out the worksheet, I ask, "How are we doing? Are our kids growing into mature young Christians?" Most say we could be doing better...much better.

3. Cite statistics about the church's apparent lack of impact on its own people (found in the introduction to Section 1).

Then ask, "If the church's ministry is effective, why don't we see a bigger difference between churchgoing and non-churchgoing people?"

4. Using the five questions listed in Chapter 2, show church members the home's importance in kids' faith development.

Have church members answer the questions and then go through the Bible passages I've covered in Chapter 14.

5. Explain Search Institute's list of forty internal and external assets, found in Chapter 13.

Point out that half of Search's external assets focus on parent involvement in kids' lives.

6. Using the diagrams in Chapter 14, explain the paradigm shift to home-centered, church-supported ministry.

Explain the differences between the old and new paradigms. Then make a case for starting the journey toward the new paradigm.

7. Finally, tell about the benefits your church will reap as it shifts its ministry focus to the new paradigm.

For example:

● It's biblical.

● It places a trained Christian educator in every home.

● We have access to kids only a few hours a week at best. Parents have access to them many hours every day.

Jump on the Bandwagon!

You've just worked through the issues in this book on your own. Consider using the book on a wider scale to bring about change in your church. And as you innovate new ideas in your church, send them to Group Publishing at:

The Home Center
P.O. Box 481
Loveland, CO 80539

Group will collect your ideas and publish them in a newsletter so we can learn from one another. To get on the mailing list, just send in your idea.

Appendix 1
Develop Your Own Family Mission Statement

Answer these questions:

1. What's the most important mission or goal for families to be working toward?

2. Why should family members work at growing closer as a family?

3. What can the following family members do to build a strong family?

   Mothers:

   Fathers:

   Children:

4. What does the family do to support and strengthen its family members?

5. What would be missing in our world if families ceased to exist?

6. How have you seen families celebrating the joy of being family?

Once you've brainstormed answers to these six questions about families in general, shift your attention to your family in particular...

Crafting Our Family's Mission
Answer these questions:

1. What's the most important mission or goal for *our* family to be working toward?

2. Currently, what's our family's overarching purpose?

3. Why do we care about our family?

4. What does our family do to support and strengthen its members?

5. What would be missing in the world if our family ceased to exist?

Now, using all of the information you've gathered, get together to write the reason your family exists—in twenty-five words or less. Voilá! One made-to-order family mission statement. (Consider having your mission statement written in calligraphy on nice paper and then framed in your home for all to see.)

Appendix 2
What Does a Model Teenager's Faith Look Like?

Knows about Scripture:

Has as life values:

Believes about God:

Has as cherished relationships:

Appendix 3
Fourteen Hopes for Our Children

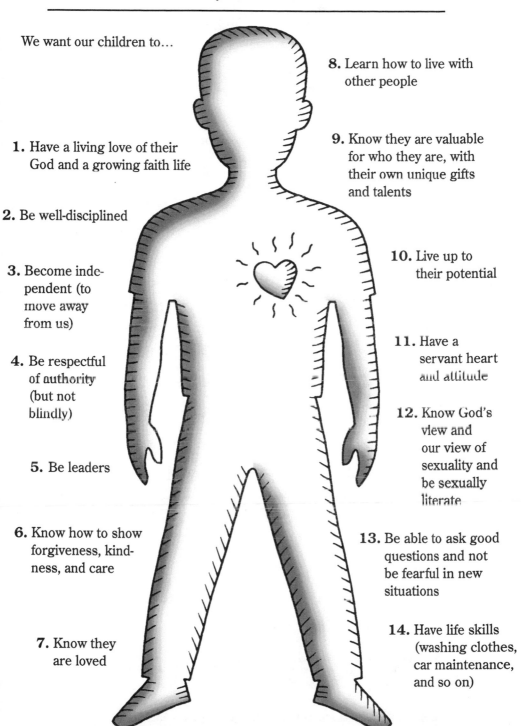

We want our children to...

1. Have a living love of their God and a growing faith life

2. Be well-disciplined

3. Become independent (to move away from us)

4. Be respectful of authority (but not blindly)

5. Be leaders

6. Know how to show forgiveness, kindness, and care

7. Know they are loved

8. Learn how to live with other people

9. Know they are valuable for who they are, with their own unique gifts and talents

10. Live up to their potential

11. Have a servant heart and attitude

12. Know God's view and our view of sexuality and be sexually literate

13. Be able to ask good questions and not be fearful in new situations

14. Have life skills (washing clothes, car maintenance, and so on)

Appendix 4
Developing a Vision for a
Family-Centered Church

Let your mind dream about what a family-centered church would look like in the year 2000...

It's October 2000, and you're seated in your worship area for worship...

A. Because of your focus on families, what's different than it was when you were reading *The Family-Friendly Church?*

  Place:

  Sights:

  Sounds:

  Attitudes:

B. Now look at the people around you. Because of your focus on families, what's different than it was when you were reading *The Family-Friendly Church?*

  Attitudes:

  Spirituality:

  Knowledge:

  Skills:

  Relationships:

  Joys:

C. You're now walking through your church's education and youth areas. What's different?

Ages:

Faces:

Walls:

Posters:

Sounds:

Place:

D. What kinds of classes are being taught?

E. Who's attending these classes?

F. What kind of building are you in?

G. What events are happening?

H. What's the church talking about; what's the main topic of conversation?

I. What's the church's favorite "new song"? Its title is…

J. What's the church praying about every week?

K. Now you're contemplating the overall structure of your church. Because of your focus on families, what's different than it was when you were reading *The Family-Friendly Church?*

L. Now you're scanning the weekly worship-bulletin. Because of your focus on families, what's different about the church's schedule?

Events:

Meetings:

Visits:

Worship:

Studies:

Staff:

M. In the year 2000, you meet a person on the street who knows you're a staff member at a family-centered church. This person says he's heard about your church. As you listen to what he knows about your church, you realize your church has a certain reputation in the community. What is that reputation? What are you known for?

N. This person then says he came to visit. What did he say about his experience?

O. This person then asks you, "What excites you about your family-centered church?" You answer...

P. In the last two years, what's become abundantly clear to you about families?

Appendix 5
A Sabbatical Plan for Investigating Family Ministry

As church staffers learn about home-centered ministry, they often ask me for a copy of the sabbatical plan that led to my conclusions. Here it is:

Critical Target: Family Relationships
Goal: Strengthen family relationships.
Activities:
1. Take a three- to five-day minivacation with the whole family to focus on our relationships.

2. Plan three special times with Jennifer to dream about the future.

3. Whenever I can, take Cori and Sara with me on my excursions so we can explore questions about our family.

4. Visit with my mom weekly over a meal or other activity.

Critical Target: New Professional Relationships
Goal: Identify six people who I'll be in contact with over the next two years to explore family ministry issues and models.
Activities:
1. Contact Les Stroh six times to share my experiences and evaluate my progress.

2. Through visits and phone calls, develop a list of people I can consult about family ministry.

Critical Target: Rethink
Goal: Rethink old ministry patterns, and explore new approaches.
Activities:
1. Refine my vision hypothesis.

2. Write a vision for youth and family ministry for my church.

3. Develop an organizational structure and outline staff roles based on information I discover in interviews.

Critical Target: Research

Goal: Gather new information and insights into training that will help parents build stronger families.

Activities:

1. Visit and interview key people at the Family and Youth Institute in Minnesota to understand its model for youth and family ministry.

2. Visit and interview people at Focus on the Family's corporate headquarters and at the Kansas State Family Center.

3. Visit and interview people at the "Father's Institute" in Kansas.

4. Do phone interviews with:
- staffs of churches doing innovative family ministry,
- nationally recognized family experts,
- denominational leaders in family ministry, and
- public school counselors.

5. Meet with and interview:
- fifty families at my church (I could do this after the sabbatical) to validate or refine the hypothesis.

Critical Target: Relaxation

Goal: Take time to rest and refresh my mind, spirit, and body.

Activities:

1. Develop a daily discipline of prayer, Bible study, and exercise.

2. Plan a family outing during Christmas vacation.

3. Have fun on a weekly basis.

4. Take two days off per week to do what I want to do.

5. As a family project, paint our living room, dining room, and hallway.

6. Organize my home workshop.

Critical Target: Resources
Goal: Gain resources to enhance my church's ministry with parents and their families.
Activities:
1. Review published materials on family ministry.

2. Attend family ministry workshops.

3. Create a bibliography of the top 50-100 best resources in parenting and family life.

Critical Target: Retraining
Goal: Research and establish a course of study for a master's degree in the area of family life.
Activities:
1. Interview colleges and universities so, within months of my sabbatical's end, I can enroll in a course of study to pursue a master's degree.

Appendix 6
Job Descriptions for Home-Centered, Church-Supported Ministry

Once you've bought into the paradigm shift and start working to bring about change in your church, job descriptions for your Christian education staffers will need to change. Here I offer copies of my job description and those of our junior and senior high ministers as a starting point for revamping your own duties.

Minister of the Christian Home
Nature of the Position

The Minister of the Christian Home will assist parents with children and teenagers in the growth of their homes as homes of faith and grace. This will happen by planning, developing, and implementing a coordinated way for the Christian home to be the primary agency for faith formation.

Homes are vital institutions to this faith community—they are the faith-teaching stations. Our homes provide the primary environment for our people to live out their faith. Our homes are light and salt for others to see Jesus and experience God and his love.

The Minister of the Christian Home:

● helps homes be centers for the growth of the Christian faith, and helps equip parents with faith-filled parenting and couple-relationship skills;

● opens opportunities for homes to live out God's will and love in their everyday lives—enabling home networks and providing Christian resources to help homes pass on the faith from one generation to the next;

● motivates the people of the church to be Christian stewards of children—our most precious gift—who give of themselves in service to God and neighbor;

● encourages families to display their love for God and each other as a witness to Christ's love in their neighborhood;

● supports God's plan for marriage and the family as the primary agency for faith formation;

- lifts up, develops, and carries out an action plan for ministry—working with the pastor, staff, and congregation—based on our vision for homes as the primary agencies for faith formation; and
- ensures that each home has the opportunity to know and live out God's will, creating a place where God's love abounds for all who live there and enabling the faith to be passed on from one generation to the next through the power of the Spirit.

Qualifications

The Minister to the Christian Home must be an individual who...
- is willing to grow in his or her field of expertise;
- demonstrates a personal relationship with Jesus Christ through worship, prayer, and Bible study;
- demonstrates a high level of Christian moral integrity;
- is mature in the faith and exhibits an understanding of service within the church and a desire to apply his or her talents within that context;
- has a broad working knowledge of church education and ministry for, to, and with children, junior highers, and senior highers.
- is willing to use his or her gifts to encourage, equip, and train parents to help their homes be the primary agencies for faith formation;
- has a working knowledge of marriage and the family and a willingness to use that knowledge to build strong Christian homes; and
- understands the church to be a place that empowers the home to take its rightful place in the community as a Christian model of marriage and the family and is willing to create faith-development programs to support, encourage, and train parents toward that end.

Reporting Relationships

The Minister to the Christian Home shall...
- report to the senior pastor as team leader of the ministry staff; and
- report to the church through the Nurture Coordinating Council.

Responsibilities

A. Advocacy and management for home-centered faith development and a home-centered church:

- Help the home and church develop and understand a home-centered ministry style in the church's structure and programming.

● Serve as team leader for our faith-development ministry. The team leader mentors, empowers, and equips as needed those who are called and hired—who have specific duties and tasks in developing faith in the home.

B. Parent training and family-life education:

● Help parents grow in their skills as spiritual leaders in their homes—nurturing and guiding their children as God's faithful people through a coordinated parent/home faith-development system and a "stages" ministry.

C. Premarriage and marriage enrichment:

● Provide resources, training, and opportunities for homes being dreamed of (engaged couples), new homes being formed (newly married couples), homes formed, and homes being reformed (due to loss or choice)—to help families to be ready for the important ministry they'll be asked to do in their homes.

● Provide opportunities for the nurture of marriages and relationships in the home.

D. Mentoring and connecting homes:

● Recruit, train, and make available "mentoring" homes.

● Connect people who have home-centered concerns and desires with mentors who can help meet their needs.

● Develop a systematic faith-development contact system for homes with children and teenagers in the church.

E. Support groups:

● Develop appropriate support groups for homes as needed.

● Support homes in modeling a lifestyle that promotes faith formation.

F. Resources:

● Provide resources (through the Home Resource Center) for developing a healthy family life.

● Specific duties will reflect what's currently happening in our congregation and will change year to year as staff changes.

Ministers to Junior Highers and Senior Highers

Nature of the Positions

The world our youth live in operates counter to the gospel message. The Ministers to Junior and Senior Highers provide—through the home and church and to the community—leadership and ministry for junior and senior highers.

Ministers to Junior Highers and Senior Highers:

● are advocates for young people, helping shape the church into a youth-friendly environment and building its reputation in the community as a friend of the home;
● shape and develop a Christian community in which young people can live out and practice their love for Christ in a safe environment;
● lift up, develop, and carry out an action plan for ministry—working with the Minister of the Christian Home, families, and our nurture staff—based on our vision for homes as the primary agencies for faith formation.

The Minister to Junior Highers:

● assists and supports junior highers in their faith journeys;
● aids parents in the growth and nurture of their junior highers' faith by providing growth opportunities at church and home through a coordinated curriculum and a variety of activities;
● grows in his or her love for Scripture;
● knows the doctrines of the church;
● is involved in service and mission;
● is morally responsible; and
● loves his or her neighbors by reaching out to them with the gospel.

The Minister to Senior Highers:

● supports senior highers in their journeys of faith through planning, developing, and implementing a Christian ministry for, with, and to the young people, helping them to gain a sense of who they are—an identity that centers on God and his church, with the home being the primary agency for faith formation.
● develops a ministry that helps senior highers grow in their personal relationship with Christ, develop a greater love for God and neighbor,

and be "discipled" toward an integrated life of service to God and others.

Therefore, the Ministers to Junior Highers and Senior Highers will:

● speak out on behalf of all young people,
● reach out to form and re-form relationships,
● train and equip adults to work with young people,
● enhance the church's relationship with the home and support the home as the primary agency for faith formation,
● empower teenagers' gifts for ministry, and
● nurture faith through confirmation ministry and a variety of faith-development opportunities that are sensitive to the home and its ministry.

Qualifications

Individuals who...

● are youth-friendly—willing to build relationships with young people and relate to their culture;
● are willing to work in team ministry on a multilevel staff;
● are willing to grow in their field of expertise and relationship to God;
● are Christians who demonstrate a personal relationship with Jesus Christ through worship, prayer, and Scripture knowledge;
● demonstrate a high level of Christian moral integrity;
● are mature in the faith and exhibit an understanding of service within the church and a desire to apply their talents within that context;
● have a working knowledge of Christian education and youth ministry and are willing to use those gifts for ministry that focuses on the home as the primary agency for faith formation;
● understand the church to be a place that empowers the home to take its rightful place in the community as a faith-teaching station for the advancement of God's kingdom; and
● demonstrate the ability to work with large groups of young people.

Reporting Relationships:

The Ministers to Senior Highers and Junior Highers shall...

● be a part of the church's ministry team;
● report to the Minister of the Christian Home—the team leader for the faith-development staff; and

• report to the church through the Junior and Senior Higher Nurture Boards and the Nurture Coordinating Council.

Responsibilities

A. Administrate a ministry to young people in grades six through twelve.

B. Work to build a program for junior and senior high young people that reflects a home-centered, church supported model—based on our vision that the home is the primary agency for faith formation and parents are the primary ministers of youth in the church.

C. Through the home and church, encourage continued growth in knowledge, love, and passion for God through worship, study, and prayer.

D. Be an advocate for a youth-friendly church.

E. Connect young people to their parents, each other, and the church faith-community.

F. Empower young people's gifts for service and as witnesses to the gospel.

G. Help each young person gain a vision, through his or her home and church, for his or her life's ministry, vocation, and avocation.

H. Develop a Christian community through ministry programs that are supportive to young people from many different schools.

I. Develop ministry training for adults so they can be effective in their work with young people through the church's ministry.

Appendix 7
Celebrate the Child: A Home Christmas Banner Kit for a Family Christmas Eve Worship Service

Materials Included: 17x22-inch paper, a dowel rod, scissors, glue, markers or crayons, yarn to hang the banner, tape or buttons, and other optional supplies

Directions:

1. Measure one inch down from the edge of one of the 17-inch (short side) sides of the banner paper. Fold that edge of paper over and glue it, making a 1/4-inch sleeve to slide the banner rod through for hanging.

2. Put the following items on your banner in some way:

a. your family name

b. the name of each person who lives in your home

c. a symbol of Christmas that is special to your home

d. a written Christmas message that you wish to share with others

3. Create your Family Christmas Banner using these ideas or your own:

● Draw and color pictures and words on the banner.

● Find words and pictures in magazines, and glue them to the banner in a collage.

● Cut words or symbols out of colored paper, and glue them to the banner.

● Attach photographs of your family and your Christmas symbols to the banner.

● Sew pieces of cloth to the banner.

● Create pictures and words on a computer and then cut them out and paste them to the banner.

4. Put the banner rod through the sleeve at the top of the banner, and tie the yarn on each end. Tape the yarn to the banner rod so it doesn't slip off the ends (or glue a button on each end).

5. Bring the Family Banner to church for the Children's Family Christmas Eve Worship.

Appendix 8
Bible Presentation Sunday Letter

Dear parents of a Concordia kindergartner,

Your home is a most powerful influence in the faith development of your kindergartner. We want to support you as you nurture this most precious gift. Therefore, you are invited to receive, as a gift from the church, the *Read With Me Bible,* a children's Bible storybook. It is age-appropriate and a great way to read with your kindergartner the great stories of the Bible.

To receive this gift, we need you to do the following:
1. Come to any of the three morning services on Sunday, April 20th with your kindergartner.
2. Come forward for the children's message with your kindergartner, and sit next to him or her.
3. During the children's message, we will give your child a Bible. At some point during the message, he or she will be directed to stand next to you.
4. We will go through the following responsive declaration:

Ben: Children, please repeat after me…"The Bible is God's Word. Mom or Dad, will you read with me the stories of the Bible in this Bible storybook?" *(Children repeat.)*
Ben: Parents, if this is your wish, please respond to your child's request by saying, "Yes, with God's help and guidance." *(Parents respond.)*
Ben: May God bless your home as the primary agency for faith formation.

We ask all families of kindergartners to come to a short "How to Use the Bible Storybook at Home" training session. The entire family will enjoy this minievent. If the entire family cannot come, we hope parents and kindergartners will join us. This is a great opportunity to invite grandparents to join you.

The training will include:
1. writing your child's name in the Bible storybook,

2. receiving a special instructional bookmark,

3. a short briefing about Bible reading with children at home, and

4. reading the first story from your new Bible storybook together. The training will be held according to the schedule below. Please note the following locations and times.

● After the 8:00 a.m. service in the gym—at 9:30 a.m.

● After the 9:30 a.m. service in the gym—at 10:45 a.m.

● During the 10:45 a.m. service. After the children's message, simply follow me to the Adult Center for a short briefing.

You will be receiving a phone call to answer any questions you may have about this event, to let us know if you accept our invitation, and to tell us during which service you will be accepting this gift.

God bless your home,

Ben Freudenburg
Minister to the Christian Home

Appendix 9
Bookmark

Using the Bible With Your Child

1. Pray with your child. Pray that your child will understand the story and grow to love God's Word.

2. Read the story with your child or to your child.

3. Ask God to bless your child with one of the following blessings or one of your own:

May the light of God surround you,
The love of God enfold you,
The power of God protect you,
The presence of God watch over you,
Wherever you are, God is.

Christ be with you.
Christ beside you.
Christ before you.
Christ behind you.
Christ within you.
Christ to win you.
Christ to comfort and restore you.

Great Stories to Read When You Are:

Afraid—Jesus calms the storm

Happy—A praise Psalm

Feeling selfish—Jesus feeds five thousand

Worried—The Shepherd's Psalm

Sad—The empty tomb

Sorry—The story of the lost son

Sick—Jesus heals a lame man

Get into God's Word!

Appendix 10
Family Bible Hour Discussion Worksheet

Bible Words:
"Serve one another in love" (Galatians 5:13b).

Today's Bible Story:
Jesus washes his disciples' feet. (John 13:1-11)

Discussion Questions:
● When was the last time you did something good for someone else?
● Would you give up something you like to do in order to help someone?
● How was Jesus a servant? What did he give up?

Prayer Thoughts:
● Pray that God brings someone into your life you can help.
● Ask the Holy Spirit to help you grow in your faith.
● Praise Jesus that he gave his life for you.

A Challenge for This Week:

● Send an encouraging note to someone.

Home Month

We invite you to sign up for "A Home Faith-Development Plan for All Ages and Stages."

What is Home Month? The church council, the faith-development boards, and the staff have made a commitment to shape our church's ministry around this vision statement: "The home is the primary agency for faith formation." Home Month is the kickoff to living that vision out in this place. When you sign up for the Home Month Faith-Development Plan for the month of April, you will receive:

● **A packet of home faith-development ideas** for all age levels, life stages, and kinds of homes. The packet has seven idea cards for home faith-development. They range from ideas for having fun at home to ideas about telling faith stories. We ask each home to do one idea from one card the first week, one idea from each of two cards the next week, one idea from each of three cards the third week, and one idea from each of four cards the fourth week.

Each Sunday, those who sign up for this Home Month plan will have the opportunity to join a Home Huddle from 9:00 to 9:30 a.m. in the gym. Home Huddles offer your family a time to hear what others are doing at home and how it's working while you receive encouragement and prayer to keep going.

To sign your home up for the Home Month Faith-Development Plan, fill out the enclosed Home Month Bookmark and put it in the slot of the roof in the model home next to the Home Month banner at church. (A sample Home Month Faith-Development Packet can be found in Appendix 12 on pages 168-172.)

These are a few of the differences you'll see in our church during Home Month:

● The calendar for April will change to favor home activities.
● We declare April 8th, the Monday after Easter, "Stay at Home Night." We will encourage all members to stay home and enjoy the afterglow of Easter.

● We encourage families to go on an activity together. On April 13, go to "Family Day" at Six Flags. Those who buy the first one hundred tickets will receive free Six Flags Bugs Bunny enamel pins. Buy your tickets through the church by March 31 for a great discount. Or, on April 20, participate in "The Family Walk" as a fundraiser for needy families in our community. We encourage you to serve the needs of others by walking together.

● All ministry boards will be encouraged to meet on Tuesday, April 16, beginning at 7:00 p.m. This will clear other nights for home activities.

● The staff will encourage each other to spend adequate time at home for Sabbath rest.

● We will experiment with home-centered, church-supported styles and activities in our Christian education programs and the worship service.

Home Faith-Development Ideas

We challenge and encourage you to:

- Do **one** activity from **one** card the first week.
- Do **one** activity from each of **two** cards the second week.
- Do **one** activity from each of **three** cards the third week.
- Do **one** activity from each of **four** cards the fourth week.

Continue using these ideas as the Holy Spirit blesses your home. May you find great joy in nurturing your Christian home. For continued encouragement and prayer, join a Home Huddle each Sunday.

This Home Month Faith-Development Packet includes seven idea cards. The areas include:

1. Reading Scripture—Ideas that encourage your home to read God's Word

2. Praying— Ways to talk with God that strengthen the prayer life in your home

3. Sharing faith stories—Ways to tell about the Gospel in your home

4. Managing the home—Strategies for diminishing stress in your home

5. Serving one another—Activities that view your home through a servant filter

6. Memorizing Scripture—Ideas for helping your home integrate God's Word into your hearts and minds

7. Playing together—Ideas that support fun in your home

Reading Scripture

- Read next week's lessons to prepare for worship.
- Take your Bible to lunch.
- Commit to a specific time each day to read God's Word.
- Walk and listen to a taped Bible study or radio Bible study.
- Invite family and friends over for a Bible study.
- Have daily devotions.
- Ask a fellow church member to be a reading partner.
- Read a Bible commentary.
- Listen to Bible study tapes in your car.
- Join a Bible class that includes homework!
- Read from age-appropriate "Bible books."

. . . .

Praying in the Home

- Establish a quiet time each day to pray.
- Take a prayer walk.
- Have a "squeeze prayer." Hold hands. Each person prays a sentence, then squeezes the hand of the next person, signaling it's time for that person to pray.
- List your prayer needs via e-mail.
- Seek a prayer partner.
- Keep a prayer list on the refrigerator.
- Check the weekly church calendar. Pray for the day's activities, leaders, and participants.
- Place a prayer basket in your home. Encourage family members to write their needs on slips of paper and place them in a basket.
- Call a mentor about your prayer concerns.
- Keep a prayer journal to record concerns and answers.
- Pray as a couple.
- Pray an "echo" prayer for your youngest child. One person leads with simple sentences. Everyone responds.
- Together say "The Lord's Prayer" and review its meaning.

Sharing the Faith

- Write your personal faith story.
- Go to a homebound person and collect a faith story.
- Recall an individual who was a "faith builder" in your life. Have you thanked that person? Have you thanked God for that person's presence in your life?
- Share an example of God's care and love over the phone with a friend.
- Call a relative and share a faith story.
- Keep an ongoing "Journey with Jesus" notebook, perhaps beginning with your baptism.
- Publish your faith story in the church newsletter.

....

Managing the Home

- Gather for a home meeting. Have family members each share their concerns about the upcoming week. Together develop your home calendar. Set priorities. Make decisions. *Challenge: Post the week's schedule on the refrigerator so everyone can pray about the day's events.*
- Set down responsibilities and expectations for the week.
- Write a personal "to do" list.
- Accomplish one task that has been put off!
- Gather at dinner for "a telling." Have each family member share an event of the day. Make this a routine sharing time. "How did Jesus shine through you today?"
- Talk about an issue or conflict in your home. Pray about it, confess the sin, forgive one another, and begin again.

Serving

- Do an unpleasant chore without complaining.
- Clean the yard together.
- Offer assistance in the church office.
- Bake for someone and deliver your surprise.
- Do the laundry together (and talk about baptism, forgiveness, and Jesus' death and resurrection.)
- Seek out a neighborhood project and do it together.
- Consider a home servant event for a Saturday. Clean up a yard or help repair a senior's home.
- Visit a nursing home or care facility and offer your smiles.

....

Memorizing Scripture

- Recall your favorite Bible verse. (Share the favorite verse of any family members, such as aunts, uncles, or grandmas.)
- Select one verse for your home. Post it. Learn it.
- Memorize the "armor of God," and say it each day as you leave your home (Ephesians 6:13-17).
- Memorize the "fruit of the Spirit" and say them each day as you enter your home (Galatians 5:22-23).
- Commit God's Word to memory by song—a hymn verse or Christian tape.
- Make a memory-verse puzzle. Write the verse on a piece of paper. Cut the paper into several pieces, then put it back together.
- Learn the Old and New Testament books of the Bible.
- Invent ways to see a verse often in your home—self-stick notes, place cards, or on your dashboard.
- Put a special verse under your pillow. Each evening at bedtime, review the verse.

Playing Together

- Spend time working on a craft or handiwork.
- Play board games.
- Rent a movie, pop popcorn, and turn out the lights!
- Have each family member pick one part of a meal to prepare, then shop and fix the meal together.
- Read a book.
- Go out on a "date."
- Turn off the TV and head outdoors to in-line skate, jump rope, ride bikes, or play hopscotch, badminton, hide-and-seek, wiffle ball, or Frisbee.
- Look through your photo albums. Or work together to create photo scrapbook albums that record your family history in pictures and words.
- Invite friends and family over to cook a meal.
- Listen to music picked out by one family member.
- Explore Grandpa and Grandma's clothing accessories of yesteryear. Have fun with a style show!
- Play jacks, marbles, or checkers.
- Play pingpong or pool.
- Go on a fast-food progressive dinner.
- Enjoy the outdoors by going on a nature walk. Explore a creek or a hill, or climb a tree, dig a hole, or fly a kite.
- Sing around the piano or guitar.
- Have a sleepover in the family room with sleeping bags. Or have an indoor picnic.

Appendix 13
Reading List

Banks, Robert and Julia. *The Church Comes Home: Building Community & Mission in Home Churches.* Peabody, MA: Hendrickson Publications, Inc., 1997.

Benson, Peter L., Ph.D., et al. *What Kids Need to Succeed: Proven Practical Ways to Raise Good Kids.* Minneapolis, MN: Free Spirit Publishing, Inc., 1995.

Brown, Daniel. *Unlock the Power of Family: Discover God's Design for Lasting Relationships.* Brentwood, TN: Sparrow Communications Group, 1994.

Burkett, Larry. *Debt-Free Living: How to Get Out of Debt (and Stay Out).* Chicago, IL: Moody Press, 1989.

Covey, Stephen R. *Principle-Centered Leadership.* Worthington, OH: Summit Books, 1991.

Dobson, Dr. James C. *Straight Talk to Men and Their Wives.* Waco, TX: Word Books, 1984.

Hart, Dr. Archibald D. *The Hidden Link Between Adrenalin and Stress.* Dallas, TX: Word Publishing, 1991.

Lingo, Susan L. *Affordable Family Fun.* Loveland, CO: Group Publishing, Inc., 1997.

Johnson, Greg and Mike Yorkey. *Faithful Parents Faithful Kids.* Wheaton, IL: Tyndale House Publishers, Inc., 1993.

London, H.B., Jr. and Neil B. Wiseman. *Pastors at Risk.* Colorado Springs, CO: Chariot Victor Publishing, 1993.

Olson, Richard P. and Joe H. Leonard, Jr. *A New Day for Family Ministry.* New York, NY: The Alban Institute, 1996.

Rassieur, Charles L. *Stress Management for Ministers*. Philadelphia: The Westminster Press, 1982.

RespecTeen. Straight to Parents PSA Finalists Video. Lutheran Brotherhood, 1991.

RespecTeen. *Effective Parenting for the 90's Leader's Guide*. Lutheran Brotherhood, 1992.

Roehlkepartain, Eugene C. *The Teaching Church: Moving Christian Education to Center Stage*. Nashville, TN: Abingdon Press, 1993.

Schultz, Joani. *Fun Excuses to Talk About God*. Loveland, CO: Group Publishing, Inc., 1997.

Schultz, Joani. *Fun Excuses to Talk About God Discussion Guide*. Loveland, CO: Group Publishing, Inc., 1998.

Strommen, Merton P. and Irene Strommen. *Five Cries of Grief: One Family's Journey to Healing After the Tragic Death of a Son*. Minneapolis, MN: Augsburg Fortress Publications, 1996.

Strommen, Merton P. and Irene Strommen. *Five Cries of Parents*. New York, NY: Harper-Collins Publishers, 1993.

Swindoll, Charles R. *Living Beyond the Daily Grind*. New York. NY: Arrowood Press, 1994.

Thompson, Marjorie J. *Family the Forming Center: A Vision of the Role of Family in Spiritual Formation*. Nashville, TN: Upper Room Books, 1997.

Various authors, *Family-Friendly Ideas Your Church Can Do*. Loveland, CO: Group Publishing, Inc., 1998.

Group Publishing, Inc.
Attention: Product Development
P.O. Box 481
Loveland, CO 80539
Fax: (970) 669-1994

Evaluation for *The Family-Friendly Church*

Please help Group Publishing, Inc., continue to provide innovative and useful resources for ministry. Please take a moment to fill out this evaluation and mail or fax it to us. Thanks!

● ● ●

1. As a whole, this book has been (circle one)

not very helpful   very helpful

1   2   3   4   5   6   7   8   9   10

2. The best things about this book:

3. Ways this book could be improved:

4. Things I will change because of this book:

5. Other books I'd like to see Group publish in the future:

6. Would you be interested in field-testing future Group products and giving us your feedback? If so, please fill in the information below:

Name _____

Street Address _____

City _____ State _____ Zip _____

Phone Number _____ Date _____

Exciting Resources for Your Adult Ministry

Sermon-Booster Dramas
Tim Kurth

Now you can deliver powerful messages in fresh, new ways. Set up your message with memorable, easy-to-produce dramas—each just 3 minutes or less! These 25 low-prep dramas hit hot topics ranging from burnout…ethics…parenting…stress…to work…career issues and more! Your listeners will be on the edge of their seats!

ISBN 0-7644-2016-X

Fun Friend-Making Activities for Adult Groups
Karen Dockrey

More than 50 relational programming ideas help even shy adults talk with others at church! You'll find low-risk Icebreakers to get adults introduced and talking…Camaraderie-Builders that help adults connect and start talking about what's really happening in their lives…and Friend-Makers to cement friendships with authentic sharing and accountability.

ISBN 0-7644-2011-9

Bore No More (For Every Pastor, Speaker, Teacher)
Mike & Amy Nappa

This is a must-have for pastors, college/career speakers, and others who address groups! Because rather than just provide illustrations to entertain audiences, the authors show readers how to involve audiences in the learning process. The 70 sermon ideas presented are based on New Testament passages, but the principles apply to all passages.

ISBN 1-55945-266-8

Young Adult Faith-Launchers

These 18 in-depth Bible studies are perfect for young adults who want to strengthen their faith and deepen their relationships. They will explore real-world issues…ask the tough questions…and along the way turn casual relationships into supportive, caring friendships. Quick prep and high involvement make these the ideal studies for peer-led Bible studies, small groups, and classes.

ISBN 0-7644-2037-2

Order today from your local Christian bookstore, or write:
Group Publishing, P.O. Box 485, Loveland, CO 80539.